# Digging into Stirling's Past

# Murray Cook

**Other Books by
Murray Cook**

Rituals, Roundhouses and Romans
(with Lindsay Dunbar)

# DIGGING INTO STIRLING'S PAST

## Murray Cook

*Digging into Stirling's Past: Uncovering the Secrets of Scotland's Smallest City* by Murray Cook.

First edition published in Great Britain in 2019 by Extremis Publishing Ltd., Suite 218, Castle House, 1 Baker Street, Stirling, FK8 1AL, United Kingdom.
*www.extremispublishing.com*

Extremis Publishing is a Private Limited Company registered in Scotland (SC509983) whose Registered Office is Suite 218, Castle House, 1 Baker Street, Stirling, FK8 1AL, United Kingdom.

A CIP catalogue record for this book is available from the British Library.

ISBN: 978-0-9955897-9-7

Typeset in Goudy Bookletter 1911, designed by The League of Moveable Type. Printed and bound in Great Britain by IngramSpark, Chapter House, Pitfield, Kiln Farm, Milton Keynes, MK11 3LW, United Kingdom.

# Contents

*To Mum and Dad...*
*Persevere!*

# DIGGING INTO STIRLING'S PAST

Murray Cook

# Introduction

S TIRLING is Scotland's smallest city and one of its newest. But, strangely, it's also the ancient capital and, surprisingly, one of the most important locations in Scottish history. It sits at the lowest crossing point of the Forth, the gateway between north and south. So if you wanted to invade or to resist invasion – you did it at Stirling. It has witnessed Celts, Romans, Britons, Picts, Scots, Angles, Vikings, Edward I, William Wallace, Robert the Bruce, Edward II, Cromwell, Bonnie Prince Charlie, Cumberland and played a decisive role in D-Day! For millennia everyone and everything came through Stirling and it took the construction of the Forth Rail Bridge, then the largest bridge in the world, to finally bypass us!

This huge history has left its mark all over this tiny place. Stirling is Scotland's best preserved medieval city, boasting the best preserved city walls in Scotland, the best preserved Late Medieval hospital, one of Europe's finest Renaissance palaces, the world's oldest football, Mary Queen of Scots' coronation, James III's grave and murder scene, James VI's coronation, Scotland's first Protestant coronation, the site of a successful 16th century assassination of Scotland's head of state, Scotland's first powered and unpowered flights, Scotland's biggest royal rubbish dump, the world's oldest curling stone, one of Scotland's earliest churches, Scotland's largest royal great hall, Scotland's two most important battles, vitrified forts, Scotland's oldest and best preserved Royal Park, connections to King Arthur and the Vikings, Britain's last beheading, Scotland's largest pyramid, one of the modern world's first ecological disasters – and its oldest resident is 4000 years old!

Stirling's history is full of heroes and battles, grave robbing, witch trials, bloody beheadings, violent sieges, Jacobite plots, assassins, villains, plagues, Kings and Queens. At no other place in Britain can you walk for 30 minutes and go from 4000 year old carvings, across a medieval Royal Park, past walls built to stop Henry VIII's army, through a medieval city, to a Renaissance Palace, past Jacobite and Cromwellian sieges, past a Celtic fort probably destroyed by the Roman army, to a medieval battlefield... and get a nice cup of coffee and a bun or a great burger or some superb whisky!

This book tells Stirling's story through its secret nooks and crannies, the spots the tourists overlook and those that the locals have forgotten or never visited. It also features some of the surrounding towns and villages. The problem with Stirling is that there is just so much, we really do have an embar-

Stirling: Scotland's Smallest City

rassment of riches. Where do you start? What should be excluded? How do you jump from the Romans, to medieval beheadings to William Wallace and back to a wonderful view? If you're like me, you don't want to spend too much time thinking about the past — however wonderful — and want to do other things, so I've thrown in all the other attractions, as Stirling is full of easily accessible wee hills with big views, wonderful wild swimming places and my favourite places to eat!

Now a little note about wild swimming (or dooking as it's known in Scotland): beware... it's not for the faint hearted! Ease yourself in, don't dive and make sure you've checked the depths first, and please make sure you're with someone or someone knows where you are! Have fun and remember to always follow the Country Code. In Scotland we have the right to roam where we want, including water ways (though excluding private gardens and fields of crop). Always leave gates as you find them, dogs should be on leads and take litter home with you!

Please note that this wee book is intended to be fun and light-hearted in tone, taking an occasionally quirky look at the past and does not cover everything about Stirling, just my personal favourites. If you want a serious book I'd recommend *Stirling: The Royal Burgh* by Craig Mair, who is an excellent historian. A more academic approach is taken by John Harrison, who places Stirling in an international context across his many in-depth works, all of which are identified on his wonderful website.[1] I've put an even more comprehensive reading list at the end of this book.

---

[1] https://www.johnscothist.com/

If after all that you just want to let the kids run wild I'd recommend King's Park playpark (*NS7893192872; 56°06'48"N3°56'55"W*) which is free or Blair Drummond Safari Park which is not, but still incredible value and a brilliant day out! I'd also recommend you download the Explore Stirling App, which is free and also features lots of me! Now if you don't have kids and are a visitor looking for the best pubs in the city I'd recommend the Settle Inn for live music and the Curly Coo for whisky! In terms of eating, The Smithy, Loving Food, Brea, Victoria's, Hermann's and Voseba are all my favourites! The best though is the Gallery Restaurant in the Forth Valley College; this excellent venue trains students in silver service, the food is excellent and very, very cheap and the restaurant has a brilliant view![2]

The book is broken into some broad themes: Before Stirling, which covers the prehistoric, Roman and Early Historic past; The City, which in turn is broken into the Parks, The Old Town, Abbey Craig and Cambuskenneth Abbey; The Battles and finally Beyond Stirling (the surrounding towns and villages). Because it is so amazing, I've given the Smith Museum and Art Gallery its own subsection. Before Stirling is organised chronologically, while within The City, I've organised the text so that you can walk from location to location if you want to; the Battles are described chronologically and Beyond Stirling is also based on geography and grouped into East, West, North, North-East and South of Stirling. All of the individual features and stories are numbered so that you can jump around if you want and all are marked either on a map or given grid references and latitudes and longitudes, but I only give directions if there is something

---

[2] https://www.forthvalley.ac.uk/the-place/gallery-restaurant/

tricky... you're all big boys and girls, I'm sure you'll work it out!

The numbering system was harder to work out, lots of locations feature more than once and you will see sites in both the thematic and geographical sections. However, I thought if you were visiting them you would do them in geographic rather than thematic order.

Due to copyright issues I've not been able to fit in as many images as I wanted, so what I've done is put links to the websites where the images are available. Who says Scots are tight!?

There is an awful lot to see in Stirling and it's well worth booking a tour guide. There are two main ones in the city: Stirling Walking Tours [3] (who I work with) and David Kinnaird's excellent Ghostwalk.[4] Another option is the Stirling Heritage Trails, which feature walks and information on free leaflets – all of which can be downloaded.[5] If you want the personal touch, I run free tours every September as part of Scottish Archaeology Month and I look forward to seeing you!

---

[3] https://stirlingwalkingtours.com/

[4] http://www.stirlingghostwalk.com

[5] https://stirlingheritagewalks.wordpress.com/

# Sites in Stirling

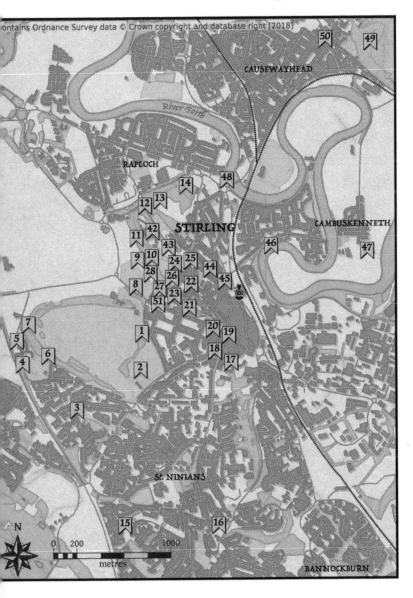

CAUSEWAYHEAD

River Forth

RAPLOCH

STIRLING

CAMBUSKENNETH

St. NINIANS

BANNOCKBURN

N

0    200    1000

metres

# Sites in Stirlingshire

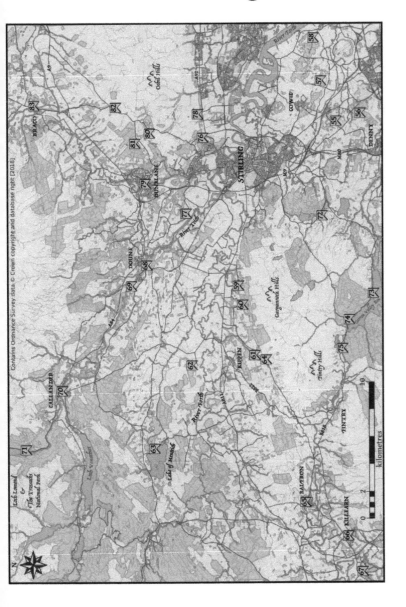

# Before Stirling: Prehistory and Early History

## Geology

No one ever really gets lost in Stirling. The castle is on the hill and north is always marked by the massive, looming Ochils. The city's main hills, Castle Rock and Abbey Craig, are both volcanic sills, intrusive flows of magma penetrating through older rocks to lie above them. This event took place around 400 million years ago and the scorching flow of lava spread across where the Forth would eventually be and flowed down the northern side of the Ochils, sealing fossil beds and layers and layers of coal. When this happened Scotland lay close to the equator in a warm shallow sea, and you can still see the fossil beds in the upper Bannockburn (**Site 72**)!

Later still, around 360-260 million years ago, Stirling sat in the middle of a rift valley. The line of

Fossil of a 360 million year old Lepidodendron – a primitive tree from when Stirling was on the equator!

the fault is the south facing scarp of the Ochils and the area where the Forth now flows dropped by 3-5km. The fault is still active and every few years there is an earthquake, though very small – just enough to wake people up in the night!

All of this landscape was sealed by ice during the last Ice Age (between 27,000 and 13,000 years ago) which rounded the tops of the hills and filled the rift valley; there are glacial erratics on the Ochils and moraines far to the west at Callander. All of this extra weight from the glaciers pushed Scotland down, a process called isostatic depression.

Immediately after the Ice Age, some 10,000 years ago, the valley flooded and Stirling was surrounded by a now lost inland sea. Fish, whales and dolphins swam over where Stirling Bridge would be. Without the weight of the glaciers, Scotland began to gradually rise, (isostatic bounce) and the inland sea began to become a raised bog (The Carse of Stirling (**Site 62**)), restricting movement and travel north and south.

Stirling sits between two projecting promontories into this lost sea, at the shortest gap, which also coincides with the upper tidal limit of the Forth. Today in summer at low tide, it is possible to walk dry shod across the Forth (I know because I've done it, although someone nearly phoned the police as they thought I was in trouble!). It is this factor that created Stirling: the most strategic location in Scotland; a place that had to be controlled, defended and fought over. Blood was shed and treasure lost to hold the narrow waist of Scotland. This military logic was obvious to every army that invaded or resisted invasion from the Romans to the Jacobites and every one in between: Celts, Angles, Vikings, Edward I, Edward II, Robert the Bruce, William Wallace, and Cromwell!

When the Romans arrived in Scotland, they described the area north of the Forth as virtually another island. The medieval cartographer Matthew Paris [6] produced a map of Britain in around AD 1250. The map is a bit funny; the coast-line is generic, the rivers are wrong, but it reflects the same underlying logic: there is only one bridge on the map: the one at Stirling. And it crosses something called the Sea of Scotland, a combination of the Forth, the Clyde and Stirling Carse. So for the entirety of Scottish history, people have looked at Stirling and schemed and plotted.

## The Harvest of the Sea

Even when Scotland was covered in ice (over 10,000 years ago) there was always something to eat in the sea, there was always a coast and our earliest ancestors migrated along it. When the ice retreated people still returned to the coast, sometimes moving inland to follow herds of migrating animals and seasonal fruit (apples, raspberries, blaeberries and brambles), but around Stirling they always came back to the coast, for the seaweed and fish, for the seasonal salmon and geese and every now and again a washed-up whale! The earliest tool found in Stirling is a 7000 year old antler pick, discovered near the remains of a whale skeleton at Gargunnock that had been carved up by our ancestors for meat.[7] At least four whale skeletons were discovered around Stirling, all around this lost coastline. The Smith Museum and Art Gallery displays the bones of some of these poor beasts. This period is called the Mesolithic and in recent years I've discovered two

[6] http://www.bl.uk/onlinegallery/onlineex/mapsviews/mapgb/index.html

[7] https://www.scottishheritagehub.com/content/22-mesolithic

of their camps, one just below Scout Head, Gargunnock and another next to the King's Knot (**Site 8**). Both locations were on high dry ground but right next to the former coastline.

The small grey stone pictured is amongst the oldest objects in Scotland, it is older than Skara Brae, Stonehenge and the Pyramids. It was made by the first people in Stirling, but it is not a tool. It was found by Kevin Wright – next to a 500 year old farm, which was built on top of a 2000 year old broch-like structure – on Saturday 29th October 2018 at around 11:30 AM, some 7000 years after it was lost!

Kevin and his core

### The First Farmers

Hunting and gathering like our Mesolithic ancestors is very efficient and very easy, but nobody gets rich and always moving around gets a bit boring after a while! The first farmers in Scotland, who arrived some 6000 years ago in what we call the Neolithic, figured out how to get wealthy. A single planted seed gives rise to lots more and then slowly but surely you can accumulate things (not that there was a lot to buy!). If you're not moving around you have more time to think about things and perhaps worship the gods. But of course if you have possessions, you need to store them in places and people can tax you and perhaps you bump into hunter-gatherers, so you need to demonstrate your ownership of the land that was theirs before you arrived. It is, of course, your manifest destiny to farm here and bring progress to the wilderness! Also, not all the land can be farmed; you really need free-draining sand gravel terraces where the land can be easily tilled and of course, before fertiliser, you can only really stay in one place for 10 years or so before the soil has degraded... and what about all these trees!? They just get in the way, and they're full of bears and lynx which eat you and your children!

These are the swings and roundabouts that faced Scotland's first farmers. The land that surrounds us represents the efforts of generation after generation of ancestors undertaking absolutely back-breaking work, every day a gamble with something that might go wrong; injury, infection and childbirth were all killers.

But they certainly left their mark on the land: at Claisch near Callander are the remains of a timber hall, 25m long and 9m wide. There is nothing left to see above the ground, but this is the first evidence for an upper floor in Scotland, as it has much denser supports at one end.[8]

These people buried their dead, each new burial strengthening their claim to the land: this is ours, we are bur-

[8] https://www.researchgate.net/figure/Top-reconstruction-of-large-house-at-Balbridie-Aberdeenshire-by-David-Hogg-from_fig2_302214298

ied here and we have always been buried here. There is a long cairn at Callander (Auchenlaich (**Site 70**)) which happens to be the longest of its type in Scotland. We think that society at the time was very communal, with no bosses yet, and that the construction of big halls and enormous burials monuments were to the glory of the community and not one individual – basically 6000 year old Amish! However, once metal started to appear and with it more obvious forms of wealth, society became more individualistic and burials become family plots (Coneypark cairn (**Site 3**)).

## Stirling's Oldest Art

I hope when you wander round Stirling, you're not glued to your phone? Lift your head and look at Stirling, which is incredibly beautiful. The urge to create, to embellish, to leave your mark on the land has always been with us; we have had the same eyes, ears and hands for thousands upon thousands of years. The earliest art works in Stirling are carved into the bedrock, small circles and pits, and are likely to be between

Stirling's oldest art:
detail of a cup and ring marked stone at Cowie

3000 and 4000 years old. There are three sets that are worth visiting. The easiest to access is in King's Park (**Site 6**); the most impressive is under Leckie broch (**Site 60**) and the most beautiful is at Cowie (**Site 57**).

We really don't know what these are for. They may mark routes across the landscape, but it's more likely that they represent small shrines, associated with the dawn or the moon rise and they are always in prominent locations, in front of a broad landscape.

## Celtic Stirling and the Blair Drummond Torcs [9]

Almost everything these days can be ordered from Amazon and it's incredibly cool when they arrive the next day, though I still like to wander down to the shops and get some fresh air every now and again! Once in a while something has to come from China and it takes a lot longer. Now, imagine you are sitting in Stirling 2300 years ago: there are no roads, no post-man and certainly no internet. So how do you get jewellery or fancy objects? If you are rich enough, maybe you host your own metal smith or perhaps every now and again an iterant trader comes round. Can you perhaps even dispatch someone to buy on your behalf something exotic? Can we even talk about purchase, as this was not a cash economy? Objects were exchanged, gifts made, and obligations swapped. The more you gave away the more generous and prosperous you were and so the higher your status – a bit like always buying the first and last rounds!

The four golden torcs found by a metal detector in Blair Drummond illustrate both the wealth around Stirling

---

[9] https://www.nms.ac.uk/explore-our-collections/stories/
scottish-history-and-archaeology/iron-age-gold-torcs/

millennia ago and the connections across Europe. These incredible works of art, now on display in the National Museum of Scotland, demonstrate a direct link with Stirling and Toulouse on the Mediterranean coast of France. How exactly did they get here, and who arranged for it? The reason that they survive to this day was that they appear to have been deposited in a timber building – probably a temple or a shrine – presumably as a gift for the gods. Now that really was a generous present.

If you want to see a typical settlement for this period, I'd recommend Gillies Hill fort which was dug and dated to around 300 BC and has a series of impressive ramparts and a brilliant view (*NS7687091760; 56°06′10″N 3°58′52″W*).

## What Does Stirling Mean?

What's Stirling's biggest secret? The meaning of Stirling! The first recorded version, '*Striuelin*', dates from around AD 1124, when the burgh was established by David I. Lots of people think it's older and dates to the period around AD 600-900, when what had been the British province of Manau was conquered by the Angles from the south, who were then pushed out by Picts from the north. The Britons reacted to this by burning down Dunblane, before being brought to heel by Kenneth MacAlpin, the first King of Scotland... and then the Vikings arrived! Under this theory, because of all of this bloodshed, Stirling might be 'Striveling'; -ing is old English for place, and 'strive' is a synonym for strife or conflict, so 'Place of Conflict'... and this one is my favourite!

A more recent theory by Professor Thomas Owen Clancy of Glasgow University looks at the possible Gaelic roots of Stirling ('*srib-linn*: stream pool, although the modern Gaelic rendering is *Sruighlea*) and connects it to the place at which the River Forth became tidal, or perhaps more likely, the uppermost reach of the Forth estuary being navigable, possibly reflecting an early harbour here.

Significantly, this means that 'Stirling' refers to the River Forth and not the town, which would have been named subsequently for its place on the river. Of course this might mean that Stirling had an older name, one that reflected the settlement and not the river. There is one possibility: a name mentioned by the Northumbrian monk, Bede. Around AD 700, he talked about '*urbs Giudi*', the City of Giudi, and he named the Firth of Forth the Sea of Giudi. We cannot be precisely certain but perhaps we don't live in Stirling at all, perhaps we live in Giudi... anyone for a rebranding exercise?

## Before srib-linn

While the main crossing point was clearly at Stirling, hence the name srib-linn, there is clear evidence for an older crossing point at Cambuskenneth (**Site 47**), and while it was certainly used by Abbots, Kings and Queens, its earliest use was around 1000 BC. Now, if you follow my stellar (cough-splutter) career, you may have spotted me from time to time on TV. In 2018 I helped make a programme on metal detecting in the Forth with Rick Edwards, Beau Ouimette (yes, I didn't know who they were either!) and the wonderful people of the Scottish Artefact Recovery Group... Scotland's most ethical metal detectorists! We found an amazing amount of treasure for just a morning's work, including an unused Late Bronze Age axe, a broken Late Bronze Age spear-tip, a Roman coin and a coin of David I, perhaps one the rarest coins in Scotland. All incredible stuff; however, my chief memory is getting stuck in 1m deep mud (please note the location is extremely dangerous and you need the Council's permission to metal detect there) with the tide constantly rising and being filmed the whole time. Readers, please forgive me but after ten minutes of struggle, watching the rising tide, I swore profusely – and then, when that didn't work, I swore again. The director smiled at me and said that it was all excellent stuff, but could we do it again without the swearing? Eventually, I was extricated from the mud, but I had to abandon my waders – which to my certain knowledge are still there. If you find them, please don't try to return them to me; they now belong to the Gods of the Forth... the last tribute in a long line of gifts!

# The Romans

## Ptolemaic Map

All of you will have seen Scotland on a map, though visitors to Stirling may be more aware of Britain as a whole. But Scotland is a familiar shape, which is why this map is a bit of a shock. It is, however, the first map of Scotland and was

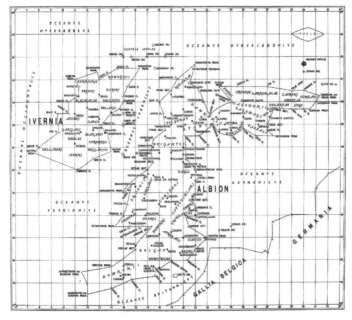

Scotland's first map: beware Greeks bearing maps!

drawn in the 2nd century AD. It was probably based on measurements and observations made during both Agricola's 1st century AD campaign and the 2nd century AD Antonine Campaign. I think it would also be very cool to imagine Roman spies operating behind enemy lines taking measurements. Stirling is not named, but the familiar narrowing of Scotland is there... yet why is Caithness to the south of Galloway? (Note to non-geographers – it shouldn't be!) What seems to have happened is that the map maker was an Alexandrian Greek who simply couldn't conceive that anyone was able to live so far north in the bitter cold and doubted the accuracy of the measurements, so rather than change his theories he tried to change Scotland... and bent it in half. A dangerous practice which people have tried and failed at before!

### The Gask Ridge

The Roman general in charge of the first serious invasion of what would become Scotland was Agricola (he's the one that fought at Mons Graupius). Opinion is always divided about this campaign: the only source of it was written by his son-in-law, Tacitus, as a funeral oration and satire on contemporary Roman society. So in it, the native Caledonians are portrayed as noble, fighting for freedom, in contrast to the corrupt and complacent society in Rome. Tacitus even gives the Caledonian leader, Calcagus, an excellent speech full of passion, which of course he cannot have heard.

‘ *You have always been free, but there is no safe refuge for us, we are the last of the free people on earth...beyond us nothing but tides and rock. The Romans have pillaged the world, and when there is nothing left to steal they scour the sea. If an enemy is rich they are greedy, if he is poor they crave glory. They plunder, they steal, they ravish, they create desolation and call it peace.'*

However, while the precise details of the campaign are uncertain, we do know that Agricola established a line of forts, watch towers and a road from Doune to the Tay, now called the Gask Ridge. This is sometimes argued to be the first boundary constructed in the Roman Empire. The first time the Romans met an enemy they could not conquer! Us, Scotland, the one nation on earth that beat the Romans... woohoo! Certainly, this is how the Romans began to think of Scotland: as an impenetrable wilderness full of violent barbarians that threatened the peaceful and prosperous province to the south. Caledonia simply became a lazy poetic shorthand, a standard trope. In turn, our earliest literate ancestors read about themselves in Roman sources and took the accounts at face value, and indeed many of us still regard ourselves in this manner!

According to Professor David Breeze, late of Historic Environment Scotland, the truth is more depressing; it is simply inconceivable that the Romans, the most advanced army in the then-world, could not have conquered Scotland if they had wanted to. The fact is that Scotland lacked good soils, mineral wealth and a developed central economy that could be easily taxed – there simply wasn't enough to steal to make it worth the candle! At the same time there was always trouble elsewhere in the Empire, in more lucrative provinces, that demanded attention. The Gask Ridge was most likely a staging post for a second wave of invasion that never came, and it was abandoned after 10 or 20 years! However, this abandonment has given us the best preserved timber Roman fort in the world: Ardoch (**Site 83**). Although it's actually just in Perthshire, but don't tell them!

Exploring the Roman Road used by Agricola, Wallace, Bruce, Mary Queen of Scots, Edward I and II, Cromwell, Bonnie Prince Charlie and so on, and so on, and so on!

## All Roads Lead to Rome

The Roman Road to Ardoch was also built by Agricola. Turn north and you end up at the Tay, turn south and you eventually get to Rome! The road was so well built and in such a convenient location that it was still the main road north and south until the 1770s! Many sections of it lie under the modern road, though if you want to walk on it, I'd suggest Beechwood Park (*NS7928792050; 56°06'21"N3°56'33"W*), where it runs under the football pitch. Pondering this always gives me goose bumps! Just think about what that actually means: everyone who ever travelled north or south walked or rode on this road. General Agricola, Emperor Septimius Severus, William Wallace, Vikings, Angles, Saints, Robert the Bruce, James I, James II, James III, James IV, James V, Mary

Queen of Scots, James VI, Edward I, Edward II, Cromwell, Burns, Walter Scott... the list runs on and on and on, and you are just the latest in a two thousand year line!

## The Antonine Wall

The Antonine Wall was built as a political exercise to help secure Antonine's position as the new Emperor around AD 142 and it's not really a secret; however, it's certainly worth a visit. I'd recommend Rough Castle (*NS8437079861; 55°59'52"N 3°51'19"W*). The Wall changes its character half way along its course, with the forts getting denser. Professor Bill Hanson of Glasgow University has argued that this change in imperial policy may reflect native uprisings in protest at the Wall's construction, and he points to the Roman destruction of Leckie broch (**Site 60**) as proof of Roman reprisals. If you do go to Rough Castle, make sure to stop at the Falkirk Wheel [10] and the Kelpies [11]... both are great!

Stirling and the Forth formed a sort of demilitarised buffer zone to the north of the wall so as to more easily control the tribes to the north. However, the Romans still controlled and exploited it, and one of the major products of this area was salt made from evaporating sea water. Salt was essential in the past to help preserve food over the winter. Now I'm not sure if you can imagine a Scottish winter 2000 years ago, but it was cold and boring with nothing to eat... I bet you've stayed in hotels like that!

Rome was a society driven by slavery, and this story concerns the first woman mentioned in Scottish history as

---

[10] https://www.scottishcanals.co.uk/falkirk-wheel/

[11] http://www.thehelix.co.uk/things-to-do/the-kelpies/

well as the first court case. My colleague Geoff Bailey from Falkirk has argued that a centurion stationed on the Antonine Wall named Marcus Cocceius Firmus (say it with hard 'Cs' – and yes, that really was his name!), owned a female slave (unnamed) who was stolen by raiders from the north and then sold back to the Empire, who then put her to work in the local salt works on the Forth. Marcus successfully sued the Empire for compensation over his lost property. Now, I am very pleased that we are no longer in the Roman Empire, that we no longer need salt to survive the winter, and that we can no longer own slaves; however, I'm sorry to say that we still need lawyers! Within a generation or so the Antonine Wall was abandoned and Scotland retained its reputation as the wildest unconquerable place in the Empire. It you want to see Marcus' altars they're on display in the Hunterian Museum in Glasgow.[12]

## From Conquest to Trade

While the Romans liked conquest and booty what they really wanted was to let people sell you stuff and charge them for the privilege, a bit like any big, bad business. The empire was predicated on people becoming Roman by buying into the lifestyle: togas, wine, cups to drink wine from, plates, forks, olives, larks tongues and so on and so on! This process is illustrated by the first few people in Scottish history, we have already heard of Calcagus and the unfortunate, unnamed female slave owned by Marcus Cocceius Firmus, but the next couple are connected with the early $3^{rd}$ century invasion by Emperor Septimius Severus.

---

[12] http://www.antoninewall.org/research-resources/objects-database?search=Auchendavy+fort

In the late 2$^{nd}$ century AD Stirling's local tribe, the Maeatae had to be bribed by a Roman official Virius Lupus (the first evidence for local government corruption in Scotland!) to stop raiding south, but they began coordinating these raids with the Caledonians to the North. Determined to stop this, Septimius launched an invasion and took his family with him on campaign in the early 3$^{rd}$ century AD. Scotland's reputation preceded it and he was keen to toughen his children up on the wild frontier, away from the fleshpots of Rome.

Like all Roman campaigns Septimius stayed in a series of overnight marching camps, which were constructed at the end of a day's march by the soldiers, including one at Craigarnhall (**Site 77**). However, our real story concerns a chieftain to the north of Stirling in Perthshire, Argentocoxos (try saying that after three pints!). After having initially resisted Severus, Argentocoxos signs a treaty at Scotland's first recorded dinner party, with the two leaders and their wives. Again, unfortunately, Argentocoxos' wife is not named. Severus's wife, the Empress Julia Augusta, remarked she was a bit dismayed to see how many sexual partners native noble women had, and Argentocoxos' wife replied that '*we meet our desires in a better way than you Romans, for while we sleep openly with the best, you let yourselves be debauched by the vilest in secret!*' I can neither confirm nor deny whether or not swingers are still a staple of Perthshire dinner parties, but they are certainly not in Stirling (though perhaps I'm not invited!).

Our final character is one Lossio Veda (probably from Lossiemouth and who presumably travelled through Stirling), whose grandfather, Vepogenus was a Caledonian who may have fought against Severus. Lossio was in Colchester some ten to twenty years after Argentocoxos' swinging dinner party, and had enough money to dedicate a plaque to Mars and the Emperor.[13] From invasion to treaty and then to trade in under 200 years! However, as we will see, there had been an earlier boom in trade and exchange with the Romans, but one that was all too short lived!

## The Locals: Celts and Their Houses

Academics are not really supposed to use 'Celts' anymore; people talk about 'native Late Iron Age Societies' as we're not really sure that the people the Romans talked about in mainland Europe were really the same as those in Scotland... but it's quite a mouthful, so I still use Celts!

Most people across the majority of Scotland's past lived in small wooden huts, mostly round but sometimes oblong. They tend not to survive as upstanding monuments and only really exist as foundations below the plough soil. However, when they did build in stone the results are often spectacular: hillforts and brochs. Hillforts tend to be large defended communities with lots of individual houses, enclosed by banks and ditches (e.g. Dumyat (**Site 78**)), but they can also be quite small (Mote Hill (**Site 14**)). Brochs are the iconic monument of the Scottish Iron Age, the best evidence for prehistoric upper floors in Europe and generally found in northern Scotland. They are tower-like structures (though not true towers as the base is wider than the height), with internal cells and staircases. There are 30 to 40 broch-like structures around Stirling (Leckie (**Site 60**); Torwood (**Site 56**), and Keir Hill of Gar-

---

[13] https://www.britishmuseum.org/research/collection_online/collection_object_details.aspx?objectId=1363164&partId=1

Torwood broch... the best preserved broch in Stirling (though it's really in Falkirk!)

gunnock (**Site 59**)) and they are all built slightly later, but why are they in Stirling?

As we saw above, the Roman Empire was one gigantic market. In fact it was the biggest customer Scotland ever had until the Union with England. Cattle, timber and grain flowed from the north to the south along the newly-built road to feed the hungry legions, all of which had to pass through the crossing point at Stirling, and of course people traded with the Romans. However, in this context trade is anachronistic as this was not a cash economy; exchange is a more appropriate phrase. What we do know is that the already individualistic society around Stirling who had facilitated the flow of goods and people for millennia were blessed with a massive increase in resources in the late $1^{st}$ and early $2^{nd}$ centuries AD as the Roman Empire arrived. We think that this productive exchange was organised by chiefs who began to build impressive structures around the Forth Valley to signify their new-found status and wealth. In order to show off their new wealth the elite built exotic architecture – including brochs, which are more normally found in the North of Scotland, raising the question of whether in some way these people were trying to evoke a non-Roman identity harking back to a free past or a perhaps a free north?

However, trading with the Romans was a tricky proposition and of the excavated structures some 80% were destroyed by fire, which in some cases was sufficient to create vitrification. Vitrification is the process by which a timber-laced stone rampart is set fire to and the fire is maintained for sufficient time (days and days) for the core of the rampart to reach in excess of 1000 degrees centigrade. The stones begin to melt and fuse and would have glowed; the smoke would have been visible for miles, while the 20 to 30m diameter bonfire would have been visible for even further. Vitrification is first discovered in Scotland and we still have one of the, if not the, densest concentration of vitrified structures in the world. Honestly, I think vitrification is the coolest aspect of Scottish archaeology; it totally rocks! There are three vitrified forts in this book: Dumyat (**Site 78**), Abbey Craig (**Site 49**) and Mote Hill (**Site 14**).

You will find no end of conspiracy theories on the internet about vitrified forts. Was it aliens or some lost civilisation? How could primitive Scots develop such spectacular technology? The answer is unfortunately quite mundane: as the internal timber framing began to rot, the gaps in the wood created flues which, if the fire was maintained for long enough, super-heated the core.

One broch, Leckie (**Site 60**), which is built on the biggest cluster of rock carvings in the area, contained a Roman ballista bolt which was up to six feet long (like a giant cross-bow and now in the Hunterian Museum in Glasgow), and was probably destroyed by a squad of Roman soldiers. The broch is 20m in diameter, so this destruction represents a massive overuse of force... shock and awe indeed! However, not all of the sites were destroyed by the Romans. Some, like Torwood (**Site 56**), contain no Roman objects and so are probably pre-Roman, while others like Fairy Knowe were dismantled before being destroyed by fire. It may be that in some of these cases the occupants destroyed their own structures following the abandonment of the Antonine Wall and the retreat of the Romans, with the resultant collapse of a local economy built on trade with Rome. Perhaps these structures were destroyed as a final tribute to the Gods – we shall never know!

## Christ's Good News

As goods and people travelled along the Roman road so did ideas, and there was no more revolutionary concept than Christianity. We really don't know exactly when it first arrived in Scotland. There are 5th century Christian objects and inscriptions from the south of Scotland, but it is likely to have arrived before that and, of course, remember that before the early 4th century it had to be practised in secret, as it was still outlawed by the Roman Empire. What we think are the earliest churches in Scotland are associated with *Eggles* or sometimes *Eccles* place names; and no, it's nothing do with eggs! It comes from *eaglais*, which is a Gaelic translation of *ecclesia* – Latin for church. The most famous eggles is Gleneagles, nothing whatsoever to do with birds... it's the Glen of the Church!

There are a number of early churches in and around Stirling, such as Old Kilmadock (**Site 69**) and Logie (**Site 76**), but my favourite is St Ninians (**Site 16**), originally an Eggles but renamed in the 12th century. This absolutely fabulous church is unfortunately closed as the graveyard is full of wobbly gravestones, but tours can be arranged if you ask me nicely. There are two surviving early stones, albeit a bit later than its foundation and only dating to around AD 850!

Erected around AD 850, the oldest cross in Stirling, from St Ninians (**Site 16**)

### The Collapse of Rome and King Arthur

The Roman Empire formally abandoned Britain around AD 410 after years of raiding from the north. These raids included the Barbarian Conspiracy of AD 367, in which the Verturiones from around Inverness raided the southern provinces for around a year and presumably travelled through Stirling. In turn there were a series of Roman reprisals in the north, again all of which would have gone along Agricola's road network.

Without the Legions, the Romanised societies that were left behind began to collapse. A monk named Gildas, writing in the 6th century, interprets this collapse as God's punishment of what had become a decadent society. Famously, Gildas describes Scots and Picts as worms and maggots emerging naked to pull innocent Christians from Hadrian's Wall with big giant hooks! Stirling, while not a part of the Roman Empire, was likely a friendly buffer zone to the Empire, and our newly-established Christian populations also came under pressure. One of only two surviving letters of St Patrick from the early 5th century AD is written to Coroticus, the King of Dumbarton Rock, who is likely to have held sway as far east as Stirling, and it berates the King for raiding and enslaving fellow Christians.

The eventual takeover of these Romanised Christian societies by pagan Angles from the south is of course the context for the Arthurian myth cycle, where a Christian King fighting in the Roman manner stages a last stand against the pagan hordes before eventually falling. This concept of the dying of the last light in the west was picked up by Tolkien and is reflected in the passage of the Elves as they leave Middle Earth.

The earliest mention of King Arthur is in a poem called the *Gododdin* which survives only in archaic Welsh, but which is the oldest surviving poem written in what would become Scotland, being probably composed around AD 600. By this point Arthur has already become a reference point for heroic behaviour, as we might use 'Herculean' today. It is likely that the *Gododdin* and tales of King Arthur were being told in the timber hall at Abbey Craig (**Site 49**) (imagine King Theoden's Hall at Rohan from *The Lord of the Rings*!). Indeed, the first real historical person called Arthur in Scotland was the son of Aedan Mac Gabrain, who was known as the Prince of the Forth and died around AD 574.

## The Vikings

The Vikings play a very important role in the foundation myths of Stirling. Around AD 900 – over 100 years after the first Viking raid at Lindisfarne in AD 793 – we were controlled by two Northumbrian Princes (you can see their carvings on the side of the building on the corner of Dumbarton Road and Port Street (*NS79656 93222; 56°07'00"N3°36'14"W*) which is known as Wolfcraig). The Vikings attempted a midnight raid but in doing so disturbed a wolf, who howled and woke up the good people of Stirling – who then chased the Vikings off! These early accounts stress the Vikings' impact on religious establishments, because at the time they were some of the only people who could write and were really only interested in themselves. While this thwarted attack was just a raid, by the time of the Wolfcraig incident the Vikings had become interested in more than mere raids and had their sights set on settlement. In AD 875 – less than a generation prior to the attack on Stirling – they had won the Battle of Dollar and were occupying northern regions of Scotland. It may indeed be that the Wolfcraig story is merely a folk memory of the Battle of Dollar. As an aside Dollar Museum [14] holds a sword that is claimed to be from the battle. Now, many of these Vikings were probably from established bases in the Western Isles and Orkney and Shetland, so we can say that they were probably Scottish... which really annoys my Norwegian friends!

---

[14] https://www.dollarmuseum.org.uk/

Wolfcraig: the wolf that saved Stirling

After Dollar, the Vikings controlled the Forth Valley and there were likely pockets of permanent settlement. Certainly, we can find a series of burial monuments in the Norse tradition called hogbacks, though they date to after the raiding period. There are two hogbacks at Logie (**Site 76**), but these are quite plain. There is a much more elaborate one at Tillicoultry *(NS 92395 97583; 56°09'31"N 3°44'03"W)*. It's also likely that the fort at Abbey Craig (**Site 49**) was refortified against the Vikings!

# The City of Stirling

## The City

One of the amazing things about Stirling is just how green and wild our beautiful city is. From my garden I have seen sparrow hawks and buzzards, I've startled deer just up from Waitrose, and seen red squirrels in Bridge of Allan. I even saw an otter in Dobbies once, though I wasn't sure if it was there for the plants or the café.

Much of this green space derives from Stirling's two Royal Parks: the New Park and the Old Park. The Old Park is the bigger of the two and also the oldest and best preserved in Scotland. It lies around the castle and was established by William I in the 12$^{th}$ century AD. The New Park, which lies around St Ninians, was established by Alexander III in the 13$^{th}$ century AD and featured in the Battle of Bannockburn before being abandoned in the 14$^{th}$ and 15$^{th}$ centuries AD.

## The Royal Parks

Royal parks were a mixture of gardens, park, farm and estate. They were to feed and entertain the Royal family. Stirling's Old Park featured a golf course used by James IV, a fish pond, jousting grounds, an orchard, archery butts, deer dykes and formal gardens. It underwent a radical change around AD 1500 when James IV swapped the residential area, now called King's Park, for Gowan Hill as improvements in artillery meant that cannons could now fire upon Stirling Bridge, so it made sense to make the hill a military zone.

After the Union of the Crowns in the 17$^{th}$ century, less and less was invested in the park and it was given over to agriculture. Today, the park is split between housing, a modern golf course and a play park, but lots of the original features are still visible. You can see the fish pond used to feed Mary Queen of Scots, James IV's orchard, the jousting ground where James IV and V hosted international competitions and, most amazing of all, the King's Knot – the finest 17$^{th}$ century garden in Scotland, built to celebrate the coronation of Charles I (he's the one who had his head chopped off by Cromwell!).

The Old Park is divided into two main zones: a southern portion and a northern portion (Gowan Hill). The southern portion is divided in two by the main road from the west into Stirling. The southernmost portion of the Old Park features Stirling Golf Club and has an excellent series of paths around it. On the south-western fringe of the Park, the path splits in two either side of very steep crags; the one following the boundary runs below the crags and takes you to The Homesteads (**Site 5**), while the one above the crags, is circular and takes you to and from the golf clubhouse.

### Park Loch

Immediately to the south of Stirling Golf Club's clubhouse lies a sunken hollow which, much to the irritation of the golfers, fills with water each winter and stops play! This is the Park Loch (**Site 1**; *NS7893693261; 56°07'00"N 3°56'55"W*), the earliest record of which dates to at least 1434 AD. It's fed from natural run off from higher ground to the west and covers between 4-6.5 acres. During the reigns of James IV and V it was stocked with trout, pike and perch, as well as ornamental swans and herons. However, we don't know whether Mary Queen of Scots liked her fish fried or poached! The loch was still being maintained as late as 1625, but was not recorded in the 1750s. The water used to flow from the pond along Dumbarton Road, through the City Gate to feed the Town Mill Pond. In 1654 this caused a flood and damaged the city gate (**Site 19**).

Rain stopped play... The Park Loch flooded again!

The loch is entirely artificial, and the path which runs over its eastern side is a 19th century race track built over the loch's dam. Looking at the pond, you can see signs of later rig and furrow cultivation dating from the late 17th or early 18th century when the loch had been infilled. The southern end of the pond was used in the 19th century as a sand quarry, and latterly for a dump of military surplus in WWI!

## World War I Practice Trenches

During World War I, King's Park was used a training ground for thousands of troops and traces of the extensive practice trench networks are visible from the air. It is also possible to see upstanding practice trenches at both the Atlantic Wall Replica (**Site 82**) and Plean Country Park (**Site 55**). Famously, of the Scots who had trained at King's Park, 337 died and 300 were injured at the Quintinshill Rail disaster: the worst rail disaster in British history. Also amongst the troops trained there were Scots destined to fight and die alongside the Anzacs at Gallipoli. Infamously, this campaign was the absolutely disastrous invasion of Turkey, which is considered a key event in the emergence of Australia and New Zealand as independent nations.

As an aside, one of the leaders from the Gallipoli campaign, General Sir Ian Hamilton, is buried at Deanston (**Site 67**), next to his wife who died at Blair Drummond House while visiting. Hamilton was responsible for the troop landings though he had no specialised craft, the troops had not been trained and supplies were badly packed. The Navy was supposed to continue to bombard the Turkish positions; however, they did not, and on top of all that the Turks knew the attack had been coming for two months, so had ample time to prepare! After the campaign stalled, Hamilton was recalled and his career was over. Surprisingly, Hamilton became Rector of Edinburgh University and a leading proponent of appeasement to Hitler's aggression, and even met him in 1938!

## The Park Boundary

To the east and your left, if the castle is behind you, is a green cast iron fence with very severe looking spikes on it! This boundary (**Site 2**) dates to around 1500 AD, although the fence is 19<sup>th</sup> century. If you follow this around, you will eventually hit the stone boundary wall. In places this wall is over 2m high and has a series of very substantial stones as the top course, rather than traditional coping stones. The wall was designed to stop deer jumping over it, and is the main reason why people think the Royal Park was only a deer park! The wall was obviously built by subcontractors and the thing with any subcontractor is that if you don't watch what they're doing you might get cheated. For instance, if you keep following this wall, past The Homesteads (**Site 5**), you find that the wall has dropped to around 1m high. What appears to have happened is that the section of the wall most clearly in the public eye was very well built but the section furthest away from scrutiny was less well built, though it's not clear if the Crown was charged the full amount!

A wee diversion next to Stirling's oldest structure! If you follow the park boundary you will find a narrow gap leading you to Douglas Terrace; come out the gap, cross Douglas Terrace and turn right onto Birkhill Road and then take the first left into Coneypark.

Exploring the Park Deer Dyke!

## Torbrex Tam

How old is the oldest structure in Stirling? It may surprise you to learn that it's around 4000 years old, located in the middle of a housing estate, and is also the original home to Stirling's oldest resident (**Site 3**; *NS7837992636; 56°06′39″N3°57′26″W*). This is the Coneypark barrow or cairn, initially disturbed in 1879 by workmen who were looking for gravel when they

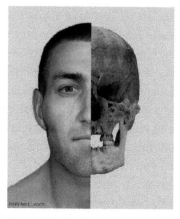

Meet Torbrex Tam, Stirling's oldest resident

found the remains of a stone box or burial cist with a skeleton in it. The skeleton was stored in The Smith Museum and Art Gallery. The mound was threatened with development in 1972 and the local society dug into it again, finding a second cist and more remains including those of a four to five year old child. In 2018, the main skull from the cist was reconstructed by local student Emily McCulloch. The Museum's curator, Michael McGinnes, called him Torbrex Tam, even though he really should be Coneypark Callum! At this point I got involved and suggested getting the bones radiocarbon dated and reanalysed. This revealed three adults in the original cist, two of whom dated to around 2000 BC and a third, AD 1400. 'What...?' I hear you cry 'A medieval teenager buried with two Bronze Age adults? How does that happen?' Well, there are three options: firstly, the workmen found some other bones somewhere else and mixed them up (unlikely); the museum made a mistake over the last 100 years and some bones were mixed up (possible, but unlikely given each bone was logged when it arrived); and three, a medieval teenager died and was buried in the cist.

It was a very big deal in the Medieval Period to bury someone in unconsecrated ground; the only reason you might do that is if there was something wrong about the death – e.g. a suicide, which is of course a sin – and so the poor, tormented individual is cast even further from God's grace. Alternatively, this might be an attempt to cover up a crime, a murder or rape victim, hidden to avoid discovery. I'm afraid we shall never know!

Retrace your steps back to Douglas Terrace and then walk up the hill to St Thomas's.

## St Thomas's

St Thomas's (**Site 4**; *NS7790193048; 56°06′52″N 3°57′55″W*) sits out of the way on its own and I'm afraid there's not a lot to see, just a big pond! But there was once something here: a Viking hogback, spotted here in the 19th century but now lost. My colleague Stephen Digney has argued that perhaps the site is an ancient chapel rededicated to St Thomas Becket. You'll remember that Becket was dispatched by two far-too-keen knights in AD 1170, who responded to King Henry II of England's exasperated question, ' *Who will rid me of this turbulent priest?* Stephen has argued that William I of Scotland, who founded the Old Park, was making a political point against England by dedicating the site to Thomas.

Retrace your steps back to the park (sorry!).

## The Homesteads

If you decided to explore the ever-decreasing park boundary you will have made it to the Homesteads (**Site 5**; *NS7791693168; 56°06′56″N 3°57′54″W*), a unique Edwardian experiment in social housing and well worth a visit. The Homesteads comprise a group of ten houses and a farm, and were intended as a response to the slum conditions of the Old Town – which, by the 19<sup>th</sup> century, had the lowest life expectancy and highest infant mortality rate of any Scottish city. The houses are low density and all have small plots of land, and were to be managed on a co-operative basis. In addition, small scale artisans were encouraged to take the houses, the idea being to combine decent housing and employment.

However, this was all a bit too radical for Stirling, so the houses were put out of sight as far away from the city as possible – hence their location in the corner of the Royal Park. It's worth noting that this was a time when miners could not take a short cut across the Park in their working clothes in case they lowered the tone! Unfortunately, the experiment failed and all the houses are now in private hands.

## The Lost Fort of King's Park

Sticking to the upper path on the southern side of the Park (or, after visiting the Coneypark Cairn (**Site 3**), take the steps up and turn left at the top) you will gradually gain height with some spectacular views of the castle to the north. On

your way to the fort try to find the cup-marked bedrock, it's a real blink-and-you'll-miss it spot! It lies on the right-hand side of the path, just a few steps up (*NS7838393001; 56°06′51″N3°57′27″W*). At the highest point in the Park there is a low domed mound with an arcing ditch around

The King's Park cup and ring marked stone

The rotary quern uncovered

it.

Now believe it or not, this is the 'newest' Iron Age fort in Scotland (**Site 6**; *NS7813793080; 56°06′54″N3°57′41″W*). I discovered it in March 2018 during the path upgrade works, and it comprises a big wall with an enclosing ditch and a roundhouse at its centre. We did the first large scale excavation in September 2018, and found within the house's paving a reused rotary quern. This represents a major technological innovation; prior to this point, saddle querns were used to grind grain and involved a backwards and forwards motion – very bad for the back! The rotary quern involves a circular motion which is considerably more efficient, meaning it was far easier to make bread!

### King's Park Rifle Club
Keep on the path after the fort and the ground begins to drop and you are rewarded with the first of a series of amazing views: first north to the Castle and then eventually to the

west of Stirling, across the Carse and towards Ben Lomond in the west, moving right to Ben Ledi, then Stuc a Chroin, Ben Vorlich and finally Dumyat (**Site 78**).

However, this viewpoint (**Site 7**; *NS7795193323; 56°07′01″N 3°57′52″W*) also lies directly above the 19th century King's Park Rifle Club's shooting range and if you were enjoying a pleasant walk in the 1880s you were likely to be shot at! The *Dundee Courier* of the 11th May 1886 records that *"The Rifle Range at the back of King's Park, had been closed for several months due to complaints of stray bullets. Several alterations have now been made to prevent bullets going over the hill and the Range has now been re-opened to the great satisfaction of the Volunteers, whose competitions have all been delayed".*

In 2018, with my excellent friends from SARG (Scottish Artefact Recovery Group) and gentleman engineer Jimmy Bain, we organised a metal detection exercise ahead of the construction of the new path you're walking on. This recovered a host of squashed musket balls and lead projectiles, some of which date to after 1886, so whatever the Rifle Club had done it wasn't enough. Stirling Council is, however, now happy to confirm that the path is perfectly free from gunfire!

Stirling oldest weapon: the King's Park Neolithic arrowhead!

As a wee aside, during the same path upgrade works I found a much older weapon... a 6000 year old flint arrowhead, the product of a highly skilled artisan, fired and lost, presumably hunting a deer... or perhaps someone, a rival or an enemy... we shall never know!

Eventually the path will take you back to the Golf Club and then turn left towards the Castle (the big thing on the hill!).

### The King's Knot

As you move closer to the castle, the features of the Park grow in significance. Key amongst them is the King's Knot (**Site 8**; *NS7889793645; 56°07′12″N3°56′58″W*), an octagonal grass-covered stepped mound, which has been described by Marilyn Brown as Scotland's finest lost garden. Locals call it the Cup and Saucer, as it looks like a tea cup on a plate, and use it for sledging in winter (myself included) and rolling boiled eggs at Easter (the seagulls particularly love this!).

Scotland's finest 'lost garden': The King's Knot

The garden has been cut from the ancient coastline and was probably built in the 1630s to celebrate the coronation of Charles I, and is the last major royal investment in Stirling. The smaller, slighter feature to the west is called the Queen's Knot. The lower lying areas were probably paths, enclosed on each side by hedges containing elaborate flower beds, with perhaps a fountain as the central feature and arbours and seating areas on the projecting lobes. The gardener was probably William Watts, who was appointed in 1625 and paid £30 a year to maintain the gardens, which appear to have been abandoned by the early 18th century.

The Knot was built on an older feature which is called the Round Table in Barbour's epic poem *The Brus*, written in the AD 1370s. The poem describes how Edward II of England fled round it after losing at the Battle of Bannockburn. The traces of the earlier gardens and features survive in a series of ditches which often fill with water, causing some people to suggest that boats were floated in them!

The use of the term Round Table is connected with a medieval tradition which associated Stirling (or Snowden) with King Arthur and the Round Table. All of which was connected with politics and prestige and demonstrating how ancient and important Stirling, and thus the Scottish Crown, was.

### Butt Well and Field

To the north of the King's Knot (**Site 8**) and built into the north-west corner of the next field is the Butt Well (**Site 9**; *NS7894193894; 56°07'21"N3°56'56"W*), one of my favourite spots in Stirling. The next time you visit, stop and look at it and imagine having to carry your water back up the hill to your house in all weathers, every day. At the bottom left of the well is an eroded hollow caused by thousands of peoples' feet, getting support as they stoop to fill their bucket. Then think how lucky we are to have water on tap!

Before you ask, butt has nothing to do with your derriere or the protestations of your teenage children! It's to do with archery practice, the targets for which are known as butts. The Butt Field is on the other side of the Butt Well. Now, this location is also where the post-AD 1500 jousting ground was. You remember I told you how James IV swapped Gowan Hill for what had been part of the Royal Park, because improvements in artillery meant cannons could fire upon Stirling Bridge (**Site 48**)? Well, this became the new jousting ground after 1500, replacing the older one which had been located at Victoria Square (*NS7914093303; 56°07′02″N3°56′43″W*).

Jousting was a key element of military training and a chance to demonstrate that a King and a kingdom were operating at a European level. Scottish Kings had a mixed view of jousting. Robert the Bruce was a warrior, pure and simple, and he had no need to demonstrate his military prowess. In contrast, James III seems to have been quite tight and didn't spend any money on jousting, which is often argued to be one of the factors behind the coup in 1488 at the Battle of Sauchieburn. Different again were James II, IV and V, who all actively took part in jousting and were accordingly injured.

All three Kings organised jousting at Stirling. James II's most famous joust was in AD 1449 at Victoria Square, where Stirling was linked to King Arthur and the Knights of the Round Table and French knights came to fight. However, while there was some pomp, James II's tournaments were about raw strength and fighting skill.

During James II's reign the aristocracy, in particular the Douglas family, used the jousting to improve their influence and sought to undermine the King. This did not end well for them, as James II killed the Eighth Earl and threw him out of a window in Stirling Castle on 22$^{nd}$ February AD 1452... ouch! This is known as the Black Dinner (often thought to be the inspiration for the Red Wedding in *Game of Thrones*!).

In contrast, James IV was very keen to show off Scotland and adopted elaborate themes for his jousts, like the Wild Knight and Black Lady in which James played the Wild Knight, whose costume had silver horns. These were held at Edinburgh in 1507 and 1508, but they give a flavour of their equivalents at Stirling.

James V was of course Henry VIII's nephew and was very taken with the chivalric prowess of his uncle, and as such very, very keen on jousting. James V also paid for a new road to connect the Castle to the Butt Field, which must be Scotland's cheapest – John Bog's Passage, built in 1531 for £5! The passage is still visible from the Back Walk and can be spotted on the way to the Midden (**Site 11**).

### The Royal Orchard

Directly upslope from the Butt Well (**Site 9**) are a series of terraces that have a zig-zag path going up them; incredibly, these are 500 year old terraces for James IV's orchard (**Site 10**; *NS7899493885; 56°07'20"N 3°56'53"W*)! Over 3000 trees were bought for the orchard and other elements of the garden and a few may have survived into the 18$^{th}$ century, but they're all gone now!

Now, at the top of the orchard terraces you can either turn left and walk toward the royal midden (**Site 11**) and indeed the rest of the Royal Park, or turn right which will take you to the Old Town Cemetery (**Site 28**) and ultimately to the Castle (**Site 42**).

## The Royal Midden

These days most people recycle. I have four different wheelie bins and a blue box for glass. I rake up leaves and rotten apples from my garden for the vegetable patch, and I always pick up litter in the street! The past was quite different. Everything – and I mean everything – went into middens: food waste, glass, pottery, shells and what is (in polite circles) called night soil, all got chucked outside! Now, as you might guess, this caused some health problems for Stirling, but at the castle it has given us an incredible time capsule: albeit a slimy, sticky one! To the south of the King's Old Buildings on what's known as the Back Walk, sits an area of black rich soil, stretching for at least 200m east to west and 100m up and down the slope; the biggest Royal dump in Scotland! This is Stirling Castle's midden (**Site 11**; *NS7893494027; 56°07′25″N3°56′57″W*) and for nearly 700 years all of the castle's waste went down the slope. If you wander along the Back Walk you will spot it immediately; it's full of pottery, animal bones, shells and much, much more. I undertook the first excavation of the midden with children from Allan's Primary School in 2016 and we found over 2000 artefacts, including medieval and post-medieval pottery and a misshapen musket ball, as well as modern glass and ceramics. A surprising find was a WWI Austrian army belt buckle. The artefacts reveal information on the lives of the people of Stirling from the Medieval Period to modern times.[15]

---

[15] http://www.archaeologyreportsonline.com/PDF/ ARO27_Backwalk_Stirling.pdf

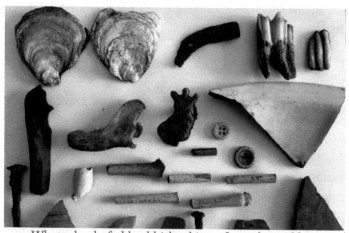
What a load of old rubbish: objects from the midden!

However, please note that the midden is protected by law and you must not dig into or pick up the finds. If you do spot something amazing, it belongs to the Queen and you must report it to Treasure Trove,[16] or you could simply pass it to the Smith Museum and they'll do it for you... but whatever you do, please don't put it on eBay as you'll definitely be breaking the law!

Stirling had its golden period during the reign of James IV, who was probably born in Stirling. As we have seen, he was a renaissance King wishing to operate and impress at a European level. He invested in joisting, religion, ship building, poetry, pomp and ceremony, and amongst all of this he encouraged scientific research – including flight. John Damian de Falcuis, or *Giovanni Damiano de Falcucci*, was an alchemist working in James IV's court. Apparently he developed some wings made from chicken feathers and attempted to fly from

---

[16] https://treasuretrovescotland.co.uk/

the castle. Guess what happened next? The feathers failed and he landed in the midden, breaking his thigh. He claimed his attempt failed as he should have used eagle feathers! Now, this may not have actually happened as the only record of it is in a contemporary satirical poem mocking him, but I would prefer to think of this as yet another example of Scotland as a pioneer in cutting edge research!

Keep walking along the Back Walk, you can turn right and head to the Castle or you can cross the road to Gowan Hill.

## Gowan Hill

Gowan Hill (**Site 12**; *NS7897594306; 56°07′34″N3°56′55″W*), the northern most element of the Old Park, is well worth half a day in and of itself. It has its own dedicated trail, several fruit trees (from which you can help yourself!) and, of course, Mote Hill which features the Beheading stone, two cannons and a vitrified fort! But if you've come from the castle, start with the Roman Stone!

## The Roman Stone

Other than a series of very lovely views the only thing to see on Gowan Hill is the Roman Stone (**Site 13**; *NS7909094349; 56°07′35″N3°56′48″W*), which is very hard to find and on the edge of a cliff... so be very, very careful! My day job is working for Stirling Council and I know councils get blamed for a lot of things, but I was still a bit surprised to learn that people thought that the Council had destroyed the Roman Stone because someone couldn't find it! Now, I can confirm that the Council did not destroy the stone and it's definitely still there! But what is the Roman Stone? Well, that's a bit of a mystery: the stone is a bedrock outcrop with a contracted Latin inscrip-

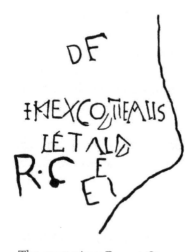

The mysterious Roman Stone

tion on it. The inscription says (I) vex (illation). Co(hors) II, (E)alis, Le(gio), (T), ala, which might be read as a list of Roman army units – but not really in a standard Roman way, as the Latin is a bit pants!

Now, we are meant to think that this might be the work of a Roman soldier saying he was here, or perhaps something to do with troop movements. However, according to the impressively named Royal Commission on the Ancient and Historic Monuments of Scotland, it's a 17th century fake as some of the letters are in similar fonts to those found on post-reformation tombstones. So what exactly is going on? As we're friends, I'll tell you my theory: I think that this is connected to the final phases of royal interest and investment in Stirling (e.g. the King's Knot (**Site 8**)), and this carving in the Royal Park is meant to be an amusing folly for the royal family, linking the nascent British Empire (the American colonies and their revolution are still over 100 years away) and the Roman Empire!

### Mote Hill

Mote Hill (**Site 14**; *NS7932594469; 56°07'40"N3°56'35"W*), just north of the Castle, is a tiny wee knoll on the most northerly tip of the Gowan Hill and features two cannons and the Medieval Beheading Stone (**Site 14**). If you've come from the castle or the Roman Stone, just keep heading away from the castle – though there is no direct route, it's all a bit zigzaggy. If you've driven there and parked at Lower Bridge Street, five to ten minutes from the road there is a graded, even path to what must be one of the best views in Scotland. To the west is Ben Lomond, to the North the Stirling Bridge Battlefield and Dumyat, to the east the Forth Bridges, and finally Stirling Castle to the south. It is absolutely fabulous and must be the easiest excellent view to get to in Scotland.

Mote Hill is in fact a vitrified fort 27m north-south by 18m east-west in diameter. The fire necessary to vitrify the fort would have been visible for miles. But who set fire to Mote Hill and when? I excavated here back in 2014 and this revealed that the fort was destroyed between the late 1$^{st}$ century and the middle of the 2$^{nd}$ century AD – i.e. when the Roman Empire was here – and it seems likely that it was either destroyed by the Romans or when the Roman Empire retreated south!

Too hot to handle: a vitrified stone from Mote Hill

Don't lose your head: The Beheading Stone!

The Beheading Stone is a fantastic monument and was once Stirling's medieval execution block, where in AD 1424 James I's uncle, Murdoch Duke of Albany, was executed along with a lot of his family following an attempted coup. If you're small like me, you have to stand on your tippy toes to see its upper surface which appears to be covered in axe marks and contains a rough cut channel, ostensibly to drain the blood. Now, the official record simply states that Murdoch was executed on a hill outside the castle, which could really be anywhere, and the stone itself was 'rediscovered' in the 19th century (hmmm!). Local tradition has always connected the execution to Mote Hill, which is also known as Murdoch's Knowe and Heiding Hill. Walter Scott picked up on this and in 1810 he referenced it in the *Lady of the Lake*, his world famous poem which helped launch the Scottish Tourism industry:

*'and thou, O sad and fatal mound,*
*That oft has the heard the dread axe sound.'*

Following the rediscovery of the stone it was mounted by local architect John Allan, who lived below in the aptly-named Albany Place. His highly decorated house, which he designed, contained an inscription saying '*What-E'er Thou Art, Act Well Thy Part*' which was an inspiration to an early leader of the Mormon Church. When the house was demolished, the stone was bought by the church and dispatched to Utah; however, a replica of it is now on display in the Smith Museum (**Site 51**). At the start of the 20th century the Council then added a couple of cannons for good effect!

### New Park: Coxet Hill

The only surviving element of the New Park is Coxet Hill, (**Site 15**; *NS7878491686; 56°06'09"N3°57'01"W*), or rather Kokishote, which is mentioned in a charter of Robert the Bruce from AD 1307 and is nothing to do with male members. The hill has a few remnants of what was a cruciform wood (the best preserved bit is at the north-west end) and was a cockshoot. Netting was placed against the woods and beaters scared birds to the nets, where they were caught. We know that the New Park was held by private owners through the 14th and 15th centuries. We don't really know who hunted here, but it seems likely that Robert the Bruce did and equally possible that Mary Queen of Scots may have. John Harrison has convincingly argued that the truncated remains of Coxet Hill are the best-preserved cockshoot wood in Britain! Coxet Hill's other claim to fame is that it is the likely location of the Scots camp for the Battle of Bannockburn (**Site 53**), but more of that elsewhere!

## St Ninians

While you're at Coxet Hill you may as well wander over to St Ninians (**Site 16**; *NS7959091685; 56°06'10"N3°56'15"W*), an ancient centre of Christianity and blown up by Bonnie Prince Charlie in 1746. At the time of writing it was locked due to wobbly gravestones, but it's still worth a peek over the wall!

# The Old Town

## Stirling's Old Town

While Stirling is an ancient location used for millennia, Stirling the city – or rather the burgh – was legally established around AD 1124 by David I. David was an interesting guy. His mum, Margaret, is Scotland's only royal saint and his dad, Malcolm III, is the Malcolm from Shakespeare's *Macbeth*. David I and his siblings were also the first Scottish Kings without a Gaelic name (though there had been a few Constantines named after the Roman Emperor who introduced Christianity)... now, why would that matter? Well, international politics can be like school: if you have a weird name you are likely to get bullied, if you have a mainstream name you won't! So in a British context, Malcolm wanted more influence for his children, so he gave them either classical names (Alexander), or English names (Edmund, Edward, Edgar) or Biblical names (David), all of which made sense in England. Close your eyes... deep breaths, and think of calm blue seas!

David is also responsible for what historians call the Davidian Revolution. He introduced lots of English ideas that transformed our economy: burghs, motte and baileys, the European abbeys and primogeniture. With regards to burghs, these are areas in which the King allowed monopolies to operate. The King is paid a fee and people wishing to sell in the burgh have to pay the burgesses... simple and effective, and of course the start of taxation! With regards to abbeys, we'll return to that with Cambuskenneth Abbey (**Site 47**). I'm afraid there are no nice motte and baileys around Stirling, as we kept investing in castle technology and replaced them all! Primogeniture is the system where the eldest son inherits everything. Prior to David, the Scottish Crown was shared amongst a series of inter-related royal families. So, Macbeth didn't seize the crown, it was his turn (and anyway, he went to Rome on pilgrimage and was never challenged... shock, horror! Shakespeare is not a historian!). In introducing primogeniture, David was attempting to ensure that his family (the Canmores) and his family alone were royal (however, as we'll see, primogeniture only works if you have lots of children!). As rival royal lines were slowly extinguished, things got quite bloody, including the dashing of a little girl's brains out against Forfar Market Cross in AD 1230... real *Game of Thrones* stuff!

### The Guildry

There is one institution older than the Burgh in Stirling and in fact it is probably the third oldest institution in Scotland, after the church and the crown. The Guildry was established in AD 1119 and I had the great privilege of speaking at its 900th anniversary. But what is it? The Merchant Guild of Stirling, and indeed all medieval guilds, were established to manage and oversee trade – if you were being unfair, you might say they were cartels! Stirling's Guildry is associated with a backwards number four and met in Cowane's Hospital (**Site 27**), which became known as the Guildhouse. Famously, in order to demonstrate to their wives (who were banned from attending for a few hundred years) that they had been at the meeting, they were given a pie with a backwards four on it!

The most famous member of the Guildry and its Dean (head) was John Cowane. Cowane was a privateer (state licensed pirate), the local MP, and Stirling's main banker. He appears to have been quite a ruthless businessman and even fathered a child out of wedlock. He's buried in the Old Town Cemetery (**Site 28**) and his statue is the cen-

Auld Staneybreeks: the oldest statue in the city

tral feature of Cowane's Hospital (in fact, this is the oldest statue outside the castle and dates to 1650). The statue is known locally as Auld Staneybreeks (old stoney trousers!), and at the stroke of midnight every new year he jumps down to dance a jig! On his deathbed, he left a bequest to the city to establish a charity which runs to this day, and the hospital was intended as an alms house to look after the old and infirm – but more about that later.

## The Union of the Crowns

In 1603, Scotland took over England – we finally won! Or rather, our King James VI became James I of England. Unfortunately this didn't really work out for Scotland, as the Stuarts simply became English monarchs (for example, despite promising to come back every three years James only ever returned to Scotland once). The Stuarts also became increasingly dictatorial, with a strong belief in the divine right of Kings, which led to two revolutions against Stuart rule! Anyway, this had a disastrous outcome for Stirling. We went from being one of the most important places in an independent kingdom to a regional backwater in a much bigger United Kingdom. The money and influence shifted to London and Edinburgh. Stirling still had medieval palaces and aristocratic halls, but with no money to maintain them they became archaic slums. So while Stirling became the best preserved medieval city in Scotland, it also had medieval drainage and water supplies no longer fit for purpose.

The streets became open sewers. Blood from the slaughterhouse in St John's Street simply ran down the hill. Added to this was the old Scots custom of throwing number ones and twos out the window (*garde loo*) – 18<sup>th</sup> century poet Robert Fergusson, Burns' inspiration, writes about Edinburgh's pungent 'roses' blooming each morning. In Stirling in 1841, one Dr Forrest describes the slopping out of waste from some sixty or so prisoners in the jail, floating all the way down to King Street!

The upshot was of course disease, misery and death. Our history is full of plagues and epidemics where thousands died, and we have accounts of guards being stationed at gates to deter strangers. Sadly, at the end of the 19th century Stirling had the lowest life expectancy and highest infant mortality rate in Scotland.

### The Stuart Monarchy

The Stuart Kings and Queens play a big role in our story and you will hear an awful lot about them in this book, and it all gets very, very messy, so here are a few key points. Firstly, the Stuart monarchs were originally a Norman family founded by

Walter fitz Alan, who came to Scotland in David I's reign around AD 1150 and was appointed High Steward of Scotland, a position that became hereditary. Steward became Stewart, Walter Stewart married Robert the Bruce's daughter Marjorie. Their son Robert Stewart became Robert II when he inherited the crown from his uncle David II (the Bruce's son), thus founding the Royal line in AD 1371. When Mary Queen of Scots went to France the name was re-spelt Stuart. However, that's getting ahead of ourselves!

James IV marries Henry the VIII's sister, Margaret; James V is Henry's nephew and marries a French Catholic (Mary of Guise) and refuses Henry's arguments to become Protestant, which makes Henry angry. Mary Queen of Scots, a Catholic, is Henry's great niece and marries the King of France rather than Henry's son, which makes him even angrier... and you won't like him when he's angry! When Mary

The Chapel Royal at the Kirk of the Holy Rude **(Site 26)** where James IV and Margaret worshiped (look for the rose and the thistle!)

comes back to Scotland, she is the legitimate, Catholic heir to three thrones (Scotland, England and France). So Scotland, therefore, becomes a French-Catholic-supporting back door to England!

Mary is accused of being involved in her husband's death (Lord Darnley, who is the future James VI's father) and, with English support, is deposed in 1567. Her son, James VI, becomes Scotland's first Protestant monarch – they never see each other again. Mary is executed by Elizabeth I of England for her part in a plot to kill Elizabeth. James succeeds Elizabeth in 1603, the Union of the Crowns. James is a bit weird and hates witches and smoking and believes in the divine right of Kings: *God put me on the throne, so my will is God's will: do what I say!*

James' son, Charles I, succeeds him in 1625 and also believes in the divine right of Kings, but he goes too far and loses his head! The Scots back Charles II, in return for religious freedom, and he is crowned here. They invade England and are beaten by Cromwell's troops; in turn, Cromwell establishes a republic and invades Scotland, deporting lots of Scots and Irish to the sugar plantations in the Caribbean. Charles II flees to the continent, eventually returning after Cromwell's death (the Restoration). Charles is a bit High Church Anglican (very close to Catholicism), and tries to impose bishops on Scotland. This, among other issues, starts tensions with Scottish and Irish Protestants. James II succeeds his brother and becomes the last Catholic monarch in Britain in 1685. Tensions ramp up again with Scottish and Irish Protestants. These tensions lead to the execution of around 100 ministers and worshipers, several armed revolts, and are known as the Killing Times.

James II is kicked out and replaced by his daughter and son-in-law (William and Mary, who were also cousins) in a Dutch-backed coup. William of Orange was of course known as King Billy, a name which lives on in Billy Boys, hillbillies, and so on and so on! Incidentally, this is known as the Glorious Revolution. Mary's sister was Queen Anne, the last Stewart monarch, who died without an heir. At this point, the German Hanoverian George I came to power as he was married to a granddaughter of James I (my... isn't hereditary monarchy an absolutely logical thing!). James II's son was called the Old Pretender and launches a series of risings (The Jacobite Cause) to get the throne. His grandson is Bonnie Prince Charlie, who is called the Young Pretender and is behind the 1745 Rising which he loses at Culloden (sorry if that ruins *Outlander* for you). That marks the end of the Jacobite cause and ends over 100 years of civil war, revolt and insurrection! I hope you paid attention: I shall be asking questions after class!

## Wellgreen

Like all cities, Stirling has lots of parking and in the top corner of the Wellgreen Carpark (opposite the multi-storey tower) is a truncated ruin of a building with a black door. If you stand next to it you can hear the flow of water; this is St Ninian's Well, which sat on a green field – hence 'Well Green' (**Site 17**; *NS7969993021; 56°06′53″N3°56′11″W*). This was the main source of water for this side of town, and locals talk about Robert the Bruce being blessed here at the Battle of Bannockburn. It is also the scene of a confessed act of witchcraft, described in what was Stirling's biggest ever witch trial in March 1659 for which the defendant, one Bessie Stevenson, was found guilty and executed.

Witchcraft at Wellgreen!

It is sometimes very hard to describe just how horrible things were in the past, and it wasn't just the absence of antibiotics that meant that even the most minor of injuries could be a death sentence or the lack of science which meant that unexplained events could be caused by the Devil. This is a truly scary proposition: the Devil is real and he's out to get you. I think the deepest, darkest pits of human hate and despair are evident in witch trials.

Now before we go any further let me say for the record that I do not believe in witchcraft and while I recognise the beauty, kindness and strength in religion, I also see it as a mechanism for control, ambition, evil and corruption, just like any other human institution. Witch trials in Scotland are really a Protestant thing. The newly-reformed kirk also pushes for a law against witchcraft in 1563. Witch trials are made popular by Scotland's first Protestant King, James VI, who of course ends up in the major leagues by becoming King James I of England. James is obsessed with witches. He writes a book about them and thinks he survived an assassination attempt by North Berwick witches. *Macbeth*, Shakespeare's only Scottish play, is written in tribute to James, and he makes an appearance in the vision of Banquo's descendants who are destined to be Kings. Anyway, because of his interest in witches he makes witch trials fashionable. Stirling Council's Archive holds a very chilling letter from James, demanding that a '*prickat Wiche*'(pricked witch) be sent to him in Linlithgow Palace for further interrogation. We know neither the name of the poor unfortunate nor her fate, though she will most probably have died.

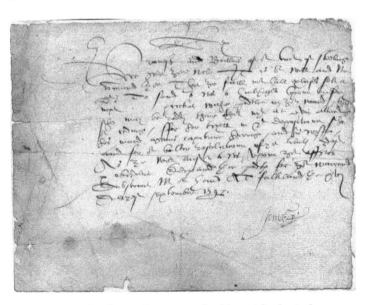

James VI demands to see a freshly pricked witch

1. *Rex*
2. *Provest and Baillies of our burgh of sterling*
3. *We greit you wele. It is our will and we*
4. *Co[m]mand you That ye faill not (all excuses sett a*
5. *p[ar]t) To send to ws to Linlythg[o]w upoun Tyrsday*
6. *next _____ prickat Wiche p[resen]dtlie in y[ou]r ward that*
7. *she may be reddy their that ny[ch]t at evin attending*
8. *our cu[m]ing ffor her tryell in th[a]t depositioun she*
9. *has maid against capitain heringe and his wyffe*
10. *and for our better resolutioun of the treuth th[er]of*
11. *As ye will ans[er] to ws Upoun y[ou]r offices*
12. *& obedience keipand this p[resen]dtis for y[ou]r warrand*
13. *Subscrivit w[i]th our hand At Falkland the xvi*
14. *Day of September 1597*
15. *James R*

Read that line again and think about the perfectly innocent phrase 'pricked witch'. What does it mean? Pricking is a standard part of witch interrogation, but we'll get to that later. My colleague John Harrison has extensively researched Stirling's witch trials and concludes that there were always more trials for false accusation of witch trials than witchcraft, so people were aware of malicious accusations (no inspiration for Arthur Miller here!). Therefore, if you are accused of witchcraft you must continue to proclaim your innocence, shout to the ceiling and hope that your relatives will get you out. If that fails then the interrogation begins you are stripped of your clothing and kept awake; if you still don't confess (and remember, confession is good for your soul – all anyone wants is to save you), then the witch prick comes out. This is a long slender bronze pin with which the witch pricker (yes, that was a real job) pricks the accused witch repeatedly all over their body until a spot is found where no pain is felt. This is where the devil touched you, and is the first proof that you are indeed a witch. Now just think again; you are confused, sleep deprived and have just been tortured. There comes a point when you break, when you confess anything to make it all stop, and at that point you become a self-confessed witch and it's game over. All that happens next is you are encouraged to drag more people down with you, to elaborate and expand on what you did. Interestingly, not all witches were executed; some were just banished and they weren't burned, they were strangled.

So, what exactly did poor Bessie Stevenson confess to? We know all about it because of the court records, and if you are particularly interested in witchcraft, Edinburgh University has a witch data base which records all Scotland's witchcraft court cases.[17] Bessie took the clothing from a sick friend and washed them at the well on Wellgreen, absorbed the disease into herself, and then transferred it to anyone she met on the way back. She also laid foxgloves under people's heads and middles, all of which was presumably to help cure disease. Now, we don't know if Bessie thought she was a witch, or if she was mentally ill, or if she had simply been tortured into confessing something with leading questions. Whatever the

---

[17] http://witches.shca.ed.ac.uk/

truth, she did not deserve to die and her torture and execution were crimes for which we should all be ashamed.

From Wellgreen, head west up the slope and cross the road to the Black Boy Fountain.

## Black Boy Fountain

The Black Boy Fountain (**Site 18**; *NS796109307; 56°06′56″N 3°56′16″W*) sits just outside the medieval city to the side of the main road south and within sight of the city gate, where the limbs of criminals and traitors were nailed (including apparently William Wallace's arm) and the other side of the leper colony. The name refers to the cherub on top of the fountain (though it still falls foul of Facebook's algorithm) and is sometimes argued to commemorate the Black Death, though I think it more likely to have been painted black at the death of a prominent local figure, as Victorian fountains are normally highly gaudy affairs. The little boy is not quite anatomically correct, but there is something there and in the past he has been dressed so as not to offend common decency – although this was more a joke than the act of prudes!

The fountain itself is the only surviving work by the Neilson Foundry of Glasgow, who are normally associated with train manufacturing. However, this charming public space has a darker history. In the 17th century it was the public gallows and called the Gallows Mailing. This location just outside the city gates was critical – people had to see justice, however brutal, being done!

Next stop is the Barra's Yett. Head north along Port Street leaving the Black Boy Fountain behind you and Wellgreen to your right.

## Barra's Yett

The main medieval gate to Stirling, the Barra's Yett (Burgh's Yett or gate) (**Site 19**; *NS7966993233; 56°07'00"N3°56'13"W*) – the one where Wallace's arm is supposed to have been nailed – is now gone. It sat in the middle of Port Street (and no, it's not a harbour; rather 'port' is Scots for gate). It was here that the Vikings disturbed the wolf, and where Bonnie Prince Charlie arrived at 2pm on the 6th January 1746 to be presented with the key to the gates (now on display in the Smith Museum) after having stayed at the wonderful Bannockburn House which is now run by the local community.[18] The reason we can be so precise is that Charlie wrote to Stirling's Provost demanding entrance and Stirling Council Archives still holds the letter. Famously, of course, while the city surrendered (and a month or two later they all scrambled to

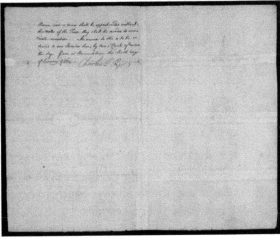

Bonnie Prince Charlie demands entry to Stirling

---

[18] https://www.bannockburnhouse.scot/

pledge allegiance to the Hanoverians after Culloden!) the Castle did not. So Charlie mounted an ill-fated siege of the Castle on Ladies Rock (**Site 36**). In addition, General Blakeney, who was in charge of the Castle, cut the inner arch of Stirling Bridge (**Site 48**) to trap the Jacobites in Stirling. It didn't work though, and the Jacobites beat a government army at Falkirk. However, the bridge remained closed between December 1745 and March 1749 and all the goods and people travelling north or south were forced to use a ferry... imagine the tailbacks!

Behind you, on the building known as Wolf Craig is a lovely sculpture of the howling wolf that saved the city from the Vikings!

Next stop is the City Walls. Head west along Dumbarton Road, keeping Wolf Craig to your left, and the walls are just ahead of you on the right!

## City Walls

Famously, Stirling has the best-preserved city walls in Scotland (**Site 20**; *NS7960093272; 56°07'01"N3°56'17"W*). They were built to deter Henry VIII's troops from forcing the young Mary Queen of Scots to marry his son Edward Prince of Wales – a period known in Scotland as the Rough Wooing. It is worth noting that Henry was Mary's great uncle (yuck!), and when he did not get his way his armies sacked and burnt villages and towns all over southern Scotland with the death of hundreds if not thousands.

The walls are pierced by dozens of holes for cannons, and would have presented a formidable obstacle indeed. Cromwell thought the city was too well defended to attack when he first passed. It is very carefully constructed on the edge of the rocky outcrop that Stirling was built on, but only runs on the south-facing side of the city; there is no wall to the north. Now this wasn't us Scots being careful with the pennies, but rather because the area to the north was low lying and boggy and did not need a wall, although an informal one was eventually constructed along King Stables Lane (**Site 43**). In order to strengthen this northern boundary ahead of Cromwell's invasion, the Provost of Stirling (head of the Council) offered to buy a drink to anyone that helped rather than pay for it to be done!

However, the walls and new ditch did not stop Cromwell's troops, who conducted a siege of the Castle in 1651. Damage caused by this siege is visible on Cambuskenneth Abbey (**Site 47**), the Church of the Holy Rude (**Site 26**) and the Service Stone (**Site 35**) in the Old Town Cemetery (**Site 28**), in the shape of small circular hollows, caused by the impacts of musket balls and cannon balls. Cromwell's General Monck took the surrender of the Castle in what is now an excellent coffee and bun shop (and they do an excellent bacon roll if you ask!) called Darnley's Coffee House at the bottom of Broad Street (**Site 22**). During the ten years of Cromwell's occupation of Scotland, one of the odder things that happened was that the number of witch trials dropped by half, except in Stirling where they doubled (**Site 17**).

The walls themselves have two surviving bastions, which were secure locations within the walls. One (*NS7943693421; 56°07'06"N3°56'27"W*) is at the back of Allan's Primary School, where all my daughters went to school. (Though the man who originally left the money for the school, John Allan, was only really interested in boy's education... but thankfully girls can now attend). The second bastion is in the Thistles Shopping Centre (*NS79731 93275; 56°07'01"N3°56'09"W*) where it is called the Thieves' Pot because it has a bottle dungeon. It's well worth a look. While making a programme about Stirling for Professor Alice Roberts, we squeezed into the dungeon with a camera man. It was a horrible, claustrophobic experience and it was lit, I was warm and obviously free to leave at any point. I can't imagine how miserable it would have been to be imprisoned there.

After the Allan's Bastion, the next gap in the wall is for the old Stirling High School, which is on the right.

## Stirling High School

As invasion became less and less likely the city wall became more of a burden than an asset, and more and more holes were burst through it. Some of the new entrances were big, like the one at the Stirling High School (**Site 21**; *NS7932593511; 56°07′09″N3°56′33″W*), while others were smaller and much neater, like the ones just further uphill up from it. These smaller ones were built by private individuals and this one is known as the Hangman's Entry. This is where

The Hangman's entry!

the hangman – or Staffman as he was known in Stirling – used to travel to and from the gallows at the Black Boy fountain (**Site 17**) to avoid being jostled by the crowds. The Staffman also performed a variety of other duties including whipping people and, bizarrely, in 1734 publically burning a 'false' book. Quite what was so terrible about this book is unrecorded though it was probably a political manifesto!

Stirling High School was founded by our old friend David I in the 12<sup>th</sup> century AD, and is the third oldest in Scotland. It has moved several times around the city over the centuries. This iteration is now the Stirling Highland Hotel and it has the only swimming pool in the Old Town, and was built on what had been the medieval Franciscan Friary (the Grey Friars) which was taken over by Spittal's Trust after the Reformation. Robert Spittal was James IV's tailor and left an awful lot of money to the city. You can see two plaques dedicated to him and his hospital: one on the south-facing wall of the High School where it sits on the Back Walk, and another on the building owned by his trust on Spittal Street which was named for him. He also left money for two bridges, one in Bannockburn (*NS8075990447;56°05'31"N3°35'05"W*) and one in Doune (**Site 68**), built in the 1530s and both of which are still used to this day.

Head through the gap with the High School to your right, cross Spittal Street (to your right is the other memorial to Spittal). Take the curving path sloping down onto Bow Street and then walk up to Broad Street.

### Broad Street

While most Scottish towns and cities have a High Street, Stirling is not most towns and has instead a Broad Street. Broad Street (**Site 22**; *NS7930303718; 56°07'15"N3°36'35"W*) lies at the core of the original medieval settlement, as there are steep slopes to the north, south and east. It is surrounded by amazing, interesting buildings: Mar's Wark (**Site 24**) is at the top, Darnley's Coffee Shop is at the bottom.

In the middle lies the Tolbooth, the centre of government and the courts for centuries. It was on this spot that poor Bessie Stevenson (**Site 17**) was tried and executed for witchcraft in 1659. In September 1820, the same spot saw a 2000-strong crowd (perhaps 20-30% of the city) watch Britain's last beheading: Baird and Hardie (**Site 51**). At the start of the 19<sup>th</sup> century, working people had no voting rights and those who had educated themselves rightly struggled with this. Following the American and French Revolutions, there was a desire for change – especially after people had fought across Europe against Napoleon (contrast this with the changes after World Wars I and II). The Government was paranoid about this, and provoked people to start a revolt in order to quash it. Poor Baird and Hardie launched one of a series of risings across Scotland, attempting to seize control of the Carron Iron Works, Scotland's leading arms manufacturer at the time (this is a bit like marching on Faslane, Britain's nuclear base). They were all caught, many were deported to Australia, and Baird and Hardie were sentenced to being hung, drawn and quartered: the punishment for treason. The sentence was commuted to being hanged then decapitated.

Now, given popular sentiment the local executioner would not perform the execution, so someone from outside Stirling had to be brought in. At the same time, no beheading had taken place since the middle of the 18<sup>th</sup> century, so how exactly should it be done? Many people claim that the deed was performed by a medical student, Mr Thomas Young, though my colleague Pam McNicol, Stirling Council's Archivist, has read all of the internal correspondence and thinks that Young was just an executioner from outside Stirling. However, regardless of who did the deed, an axe had to be specially made and Young had to wear a big hooded cloak. Both the axe and Young's cloak are in the Smith Museum.

Young was offered £20 for his services, a very large sum of money at the time.

A number of things resulted from this. The first is that in 1822 George IV visited Scotland, the first time a monarch had come north since the 1630s... wow, all it took was an armed revolt! At this visit George was presented with his own kilt, and the tartan industry was invented (**Site 51**). Hmm... I wonder if the two events were connected? Secondly, in 1832 the Scottish Reform Act was passed, which increased the number of voters from 0.2% of the Scottish population to 13% of it (ie 5000 to 65,000!). Thirdly, in 1835 all of those who had been deported were given an absolute pardon. Finally, it's worth noting that Young died without having been paid, and there are letters in the archives from his widow asking for the £20!

To the south and behind the Tolbooth is the Old Town Jail.

## Old Town Jail

The Old Town Jail (**Site 23**; NS7923793622; 56°07′12″N3°56′38″W) is not really a secret, but it is certainly worth a visit. Its construction marked the transition in society from detention while you awaited (usually) physical punishment, to deprivation of liberty as the punishment itself. These physical punishments all seem very extreme to our modern society: lugging (your ear nailed to a post and things thrown at you), jougs (chained by the neck and things thrown at you (**Site 65**)), hanging, birching (whipping with birch sticks) and the branks, or scold's bridle. This last device was a humiliating mask worn over the face, stopping the offender speaking. These are sometimes associated with witchcraft, but in Stir-

Crime and punishment!

ling tended to be for so-called 'uppity women' who criticized their social betters.

John Harrison has conducted extensive research into Stirling's branks and has revealed that between 1600 and 1722, forty-four women were punished with the branks and a further 106 were threatened with it. The branks was a very flexible punishment; they could be worn or carried for differing periods of time depending on the 'crime'. You might also walk around the city to subject yourselves to public pillory and shame.

What is perhaps most surprising is what people were punished for, which often appears to have been simple name calling: a typical insult might be to call someone '*a clarty-arsed bitch*' or perhaps say '*I care not a fart for the magistrates*'. We've all heard worse on a Saturday night and no one would dream of involving the authorities, but society was more rigid in the past and people had to know their place. Thank goodness we now live in a society where my daughters can speak however they want, to whomsoever they want.

Head to the top of Broad Street for Mar's Wark.

## Mar's Wark

Mar's Wark (**Site 24**; *NS7923093749; 56°07'16"N3°56'39"W*) has nothing to do with the planet or the Roman God of War; pay attention to that possessive apostrophe! This is the Earl of Mar's Wark, which is medieval Scots for work. Now, some people argue it acquired this name when it became Stirling's work house, but 'wark' also means building in medieval Scots, so it's more likely to mean The Earl of Mar's Work or Building. However, no other building in Stirling so clearly reflects the decline in our status from the Medieval Period to the 19<sup>th</sup> century!

When Stirling was a favourite of the Stuart Kings and Queens, it became the de facto centre of Government. It was therefore essential that the aristocracy had residences in Stirling, although the Earl of Mar was also the hereditary keeper of Stirling Castle. As the building sits at the top of Broad

The battered jewel of Broad Street: Mar's Wark

Street it would have been seen by everyone who visited the castle, creating a powerful symbol of the Earl's good taste and wealth. As a side note, it's worth noting that the current Earl of Mar, the descendant of the one that built this, sits in the House of Lords (hoorah for the aristocracy).

The building was constructed from the remains of Cambuskenneth Abbey (**Site 47**) in the 16<sup>th</sup> century, and if you go inside you will see a reused consecration cross. Enter from the rear and go to the most northerly window, then turn around with your back to the window and look down... there it is, reused as part of an internal wall. As to why Cambuskenneth Abbey was demolished, well, Scotland had just had a religious revolution called the Reformation where the riches and wealth of the Catholic church were stripped away, and we adopted an austere version of the Protestant faith called Presbyterianism.

Some argue that this building was never finished, but there are records of timber being sold from the garden to the rear (now part of the graveyard) which you don't do unless the building is completed. The ground floor was likely shops and the upper floor with the very big windows (glass was very expensive) was where the owners lived. The building should be harled a bright colour (like the Great Hall in the Castle (**Site 42**)) and the statues painted gaudy colours like the Stirling Heads in the Palace. Take time to look at the front. You will see the Scottish Coat of Arms, gun loops at the bottom (a good way to get rid of door to door salesmen) and a figure that looks like a mummy. This is sometime described as Jeanie Dark, a corruption of Joan of Arc, who was of course a French Catholic symbol of resistance to England. Now, this might be a very interesting public symbol of political leanings but remember Stirling was no longer Catholic and it's more likely that the figure is just a corpse, reminding people that their time on earth is short and so they should repent of their sins! You will also see a series of mottoes around the building all in medieval Scots. The one above the south door can be translated as '*I pray all looks on the lodging with gentle eye to give their judging.*' The one on the north tower reads '*The more I stand on open height, my faults more subject are to sight*' (the more I show off, the more chance I'll be found out!). My favourite is round the back, though: *Youth speak forth and spare nothing; consider well and care nothing* (young man,[19] say your mind, leave nothing out, think about what you've said but don't worry about the consequences).

The streets outside the building were once the scene of a gun fight which resulted in the successful assassination of Scotland's head of state. Mathew Lennox, the 4th Earl of Essex was Mary Queen of Scots' father-in-law. Following the death of Lord Darnley (Mathew's son) at 21 in 1567, Mary was forced to abdicate in an English-Protestant backed coup (Mary was Catholic and backed by the French) and replaced within months with the infant James, who was crowned in the Church of the Holy Rude (**Site 26**) in 1567. Mary fled to England and while she was held there, her supporters started a Civil War to win back the crown.

In 1570, Mathew became regent for his grandson, the infant King James VI, and during the course of the Civil War with Mary's supporters he was shot in a raid on Stirling on the 4th September 1571 and died of his wounds within four hours, probably inside Mar's Wark. While early reports suggested he was killed by his own men, the blame was eventually placed – rightly or wrongly – on Mary's shoulders. Of

---

[19] At this point no one would think of a woman speaking out.

course, this meant James' mother could be accused of the death of both his father and grandfather; not a recipe for a happy childhood, and might explain why he was a bit odd!

The building appears to have been heavily damaged in 1746 during Bonnie Prince Charlie's siege of Stirling Castle (**Site 36**) (the last one ever), though whether it was dismantled by the Jacobites or hit by cannon fire is not quite clear! Certainly, the Jacobites did blow up the ancient St Ninian's kirk (**Site 16**). There wasn't enough money to repair or replace Mar's Wark, and it was left to go to rack and ruin!

Argyll's Lodging is up the hill on the right from Mar's Wark but I'd recommend heading down the hill to the Church of the Holy Rude.

### Argyll's Lodging

Argyll's Lodging (**Site 25**; *NS7924593811; 56°07'18"N3°56'38"W*) is another non-secret and if you have bought a ticket to the Castle you will get free entry into what is the finest and best preserved 17$^{th}$ century mansion in Scotland, though its origins lies in the 16$^{th}$ century. Both the 8$^{th}$ Earl and the 9$^{th}$ Earl ended up being executed by the final two Stuart monarchs. The 8$^{th}$ Earl was a supporter of Cromwell and was executed by Charles II at his restoration to the crown and the 9$^{th}$ Earl by James II, who had become increasingly Catholic and was opposed by the Protestant aristocracy. Eventually, James II is replaced by his daughter and son-in-law (William and Mary) who were absolutely, no shadow of a doubt, dyed-in-the-wool hard-core Protestants.

### Church of the Holy Rude

The Church or Kirk of the Holy Rude (Holy Rude is an archaic term for Christ's Cross) (**Site 26**; *NS7918993696,*

Worship with Kings and Queens: Church of the Holy Rude

$56°07'14''N 3°56'41''W$) is the second oldest building in Stirling after the Castle and an absolutely incredible 500 year old church. It has an awe-inspiring original roof, and when you're looking up keep your eyes peeled for the angel! The church is run by volunteers, so if you do go please give a generous dona-tion. The church was originally Catholic and following a fire may have been repaired as act of penance by James IV for the role he played in his father's death (who is buried at Cam-buskenneth Abbey (**Site 47**). The church also held the first Protestant coronation in Scotland – that of James VI – and will have seen Mary Queen of Scots worship and John Knox preach (indeed, he stood in the pulpit).

Outside the church are a series of niches which should have statues in them. Now, depending on your point of view, these were either for idols or icons. But their destruction – along with thousands of others across Scotland – during the Reformation was an act of vandalism worthy of the Taliban or Islamic State. To the left of the main door is the remains of one of the piscinas from a now-destroyed external chapel.

When we excavated here, we found the floor of the chapel along with lots of lots of charnel (bits of disturbed bodies!) and an aggrieved local called the police on us, saying there were grave robbers in the church!

Stand back and look up at the tower and you can see clusters of musket ball impacts caused by Cromwell's siege of the Castle in 1651. If you walk left around the tower till you are to its west, look first at the ground to see the footings of a now-blocked-up doorway and then look up to the third narrow window and look for the cluster of musket ball impacts... obviously a sniper was operating out of the window and they were trying very hard to hit him! Carry on walking round to the left; the sunken area is the former Queen Margaret Chapel. The chapel was named for Margaret, the wife of James IV of Scotland and the brother of Henry VIII of England. It was this marriage that eventually ended up with James VI getting the throne of England.

The most famous minister of the church was James Guthrie, who stood up to Cromwell (who described Guthrie as 'the small man who wouldn't bend'), although he fell foul of Charles I who executed him in 1661. His statue is in the Old Town Cemetery (**Site 28**; *NS7918393760; 56°07'16"N3°56'42"W*) overlooking Mar's Wark (**Site 24**).

## Cowane's Hospital

Opposite the Church of the Holy Rude is Cowane's Hospital (**Site 27**; *NS7917593684; 56°07'14"N3°56'42"W*). Warning! Cowane's Hospital is not an A&E and you won't find nurses and doctors there. What you will discover is Scotland's best-preserved Late Medieval alms house, Scotland's oldest playable bowling green and two cannons which we acquired from the Russian Czar (he wasn't happy)! Cowane's Hospital was built in 1637, following a bequest from John Cowane who left a vast sum of money to the city, with his brother topping it up to the equivalent of £3,000,000 today. The building was an alms house for members of the Guildry (see above) who fell on hard times, i.e. an old folks home. But it was all rather austere; lots of prayer and so on. Within a few years of opening another rule was added... no alcohol. Eventually, the alms house was abandoned and the Guildry used it for meetings.

The bowling green which was part of the alms house, is the oldest playable bowling green in Scotland (although no one plays on it anymore!). It's not the oldest bowling green, as there one older in Haddington, but that's no longer playable as they put a monument celebrating its antiquity in the middle!

There are six cannons in the city: these two, the two on Mote Hill (**Site 14**) and two at the bottom of Broad Street – all of them polished by a thousand children's bottoms! These are not attempts to control an unruly population, but celebrations of Stirling's military connections. While the Mote Hill and Broad Street cannons are just military surplus, the Cowane's pair are military booty. We captured them from the Russian Empire during the siege of Sebastopol in 1855, the key event of the Crimean campaign. This war was made famous by Tennyson's poem *The Charge of the Light Brigade*, which describes their valour as they rode to certain death following poor decisions by the command: '*theirs not to make reply, theirs not to reason why, theirs but to do and die*.'

Both cannons feature the double-headed eagle of the Romanovs, the Czars of the Russian Empire. The symbol is ancient and goes back to the Byzantium Empire (the eastern Roman Empire), which only finally fell in the middle of the 15th century.

It is sometimes said that the cannons were made by The Carron Iron Works in Falkirk and sold to the Russians. Though, while they were landed at Grangemouth, they were certainly made in Russia. However, this legend has some truth in it; the company supplied weapons to the early United States of America and these were used against British troops in the 1812 war, when we famously set fire to the White House. In addition, the son-in-law of one of the founders, Charles Gascoigne, left for Russia taking trade secrets with him, to make cannons for the Czarina, Catherine the Great in 1786, and did not return... but then again he would not have been welcome!

### Cemetery

I think the Old Town Cemetery (**Site 28**; *NS7913593741; 56°07'16"N3°56'44"W*) is the absolute jewel of the city. William Wordsworth said he knew of '*no sweeter cemetery in all our wanderings than that of Stirling*'. There are actually four

Stirling's jewel: the Old Town Cemetery

different parts to it: the medieval higgledy-piggledy one, the ornate Victorian Valley cemetery with the statues of Protestant reformers and martyrs, the Drummond Pleasure Ground (the one with the pyramid) and then the 20<sup>th</sup> century Snowden Cemetery.

There is an incredible amount of history in the cemetery: the oldest stone dates from 1579, it features grave robbing, the world's first female archaeologist, a memorial to a Titanic hero, Butch Cassidy's great uncle and Bonnie Prince Charlie! If you like cemeteries (don't we all? Not just goths and emos!), I'd suggest you get *Stirling's Talking Stones*, which you can get from the Church of the Holy Rude (**Site 26**) and which is full of fascinating stories about the cemetery. Of course, you can just wander about and take in the various carvings... if you do, you're sure to spot a skull and crossbones, but there are no pirates here (although John Cowane was a privateer).

In the past, there were no restrictions on how many people could be buried in a cemetery and so gradually the ground level increased; a process called grave creep. When you dug a new grave you inevitably disturbed the previous occupant. These disarticulated human remains are known as charnel (hence charnel house) and the most recognisable elements are skulls. Famously, in Shakespeare's *Hamlet*, the prince passes a newly-dug grave, picks up a disturbed skull and says, '*Alas, poor Yorick...*' After skulls, the long bones of legs and arms are the most recognisable. So skulls and long bones are depicted on grave stones to remind mourners that they too will die and end up as merely bones, so they should repent, for time is running out – which of course leads to depictions of hour glasses! Given the association with death, this may have led pirates to adopt the symbol and of course it currently appears as a warning on toxic substances. But there are no poisons in the cemetery, and so no reason not to wander about! If you go for a wander, you'll see other symbols representing metal smiths (hammer and crown); maltmen and bakers (crossed spades under a wheatsheaf); tailors (irons and scissors), and so on. There are also a handful of pagan images: green men, figures from older mythology associated with wild nature spirits; they have plants for hair and feature fronds from their mouths. There is even an ouroborous: an ancient symbol of a snake or serpent eating its own tail on the back of the Service Stone (**Site 35**)!

### Formal Cemetery Tour
However, if you want a formal tour, the key stones and locations are listed below in order with directions:

### The Reverend John Russel's Grave
From the Church of the Holy Rude, the cemetery has two sets of steps into it, the ones closest to the kirk are right next to Russel's grave (**Site 29**). Our National Bard, Robert Burns, was always keen to tease people in authority and famously lampooned Russel, who was the minister at the Church of the Holy Rude (**Site 26**) between 1800 and 1817. Burns describes Russel's loud voice as follows:

> '*His piercing words, like Highlan' swords,*
> *Divide the joints and' marrow*'

His voice was so loud it would literally split bodies apart! However, he goes on to describe the sermons as sending half the congregation to sleep. His family were so impressed that they quoted the verse on the back of his tomb, but only the bit about his loud voice!

## John Cowane

John Cowane's grave (**Site 30**) is marked by a small iron fence of thistles, just round the corner from Russel's grave.

After this grave head to the south-east corner, closest to Cowane's Hospital (**Site 27**), where you will spot a gap in the corner of the cemetery.

## Watch House

This is the location of the 19$^{\text{th}}$ century Watch House (**Site 31**), built to deter grave robbers, and my friend Therese McCormick and I dug here in 2016 and uncovered its foundations. Why, you ask, would anyone want to steal a corpse? Well, medical students needed to dissect corpses for their training and there weren't enough of them, so they decided to take matters into their own hands. In Edinburgh, Burke and Hare famously took it one stage further and started murdering people... certainly, there's no better way to get a fresh corpse!

Eventually, the 1832 Anatomy Act halted grave robbing by ensuring there were enough bodies of executed criminals to go around. So there was no more need to protect the recently deceased and they were left to slumber in peace!

Next, with the church behind you, head into the cemetery to the only wall monument which is just ahead of you on the left. This is the Sconce Plot, which dates to 1689. With your back to this monument, walk towards the obelisk monument to the Bairds, turn right there and just ahead of you is the Gibb Plot comprising five stones in a gravel bed.

## The Oldest Stone

The Gibb Plot features the cemetery's oldest stone (**Site 32**), dating to 1579, and featuring a pick, mallet and chisel indicat-

The Gibb Plot and the oldest stone

ing a miner or quarryman. The plot was used by his descendants until the 1950s.

Return to the Sconce Plot, face it and turn right towards the cast iron cross with the decorative foliage and stop at the row of stones behind it, turn right and head towards the fifth stone, the John MacFarlane Monument.

## Butch Cassidy

If you're Scottish or have ever visited our wonderful country before, you will know that everything good in the world is Scottish and not just haggis and whisky! From TV to penicillin, from tyres to tarmac, from capitalism to the telephone, chloroform to the historical novel and everything in-between! And of course, we must also claim Butch Cassidy (but not the Sundance Kid!). This is the grave of John MacFarlane (**Site 33**), whose widow and children emigrated to America in the 1850s and whose great-nephew was Robert Leroy Parker, better known as Butch Cassidy, the horse thief, cattle rustler, bank robber and well known Paul Newman impersonator! What do you mean that's a bit tenuous? This is Stirling.... we print the legend!

As an aside, I recently asked a party of American teachers on holiday in Stirling if they wanted to see the grave. They all said yes and were very impressed at the violent nature of John MacFarlane, and who they exclaimed with hushed awe was *born killin'.* Ah... I explained that should be born Killin (pronounced Ki-llin), a small village to the north-west!

Keep heading along this row to the end where there is a horizontal slab, then turn right and head towards the stone with the backwards number four and two skulls with hour glasses on it. This is the rear of Mary Stevenson's monument.

## Mary Stevenson

The front of this stone features death as a grave robber strik-

ing down a maiden and is a 17<sup>th</sup> century stone reused in the 19<sup>th</sup> century (**Site 34**). The simple inscription reads 1823, and J L and H S commemorates James Livingston and his wife Helen Stevenson (wives did not take their hus-band's names at this point). Initials were cheaper than full inscrip-tions, but what was even cheaper is no inscription at all. Helen's sister Mary was also buried here on 16<sup>th</sup> November 1822, but not for long. Her corpse was dug up by grave rob-bers for local medical stu-dent John Forrest so he

Buried here but not at rest:
Mary Stevenson's robbed grave

could perform a dissection. Though they were caught, the subsequent trial was botched, John Forrest escaped to the continent and the grave robbers were released. There was a riot in response, and troops were called from the Castle to suppress the crowd – though shots were fired, there were no serious injuries. Eventually John Forrest received a royal pardon, joined the military and became honorary physician to Queen Victoria! The fate of poor Mary Stevenson remains unknown, as she was never recovered.

With your back to this stone, go to the tall stone with the elaborate carving.

### The Service Stone

The Service Stone (**Site 35**) is the second-oldest stone in the cemetery and dates to 1636. It was built by John Service as a memorial to his dad, though Service was a mason so the impressively carved stone was also an advert for his services! The elaborate carvings are a scene from the book of Job in the Bible, and one features the ouroborous as a frame; a snake eating its tail and a symbol of rebirth. The base stone is like a coffin, with the head at the south end, hands to the east and west and feet at the north end! But what makes the stone really cool are the series of musket ball impacts across both sides of the stone from a gunfight during the 1651 Cromwellian siege of the Castle.

With your back to the Church of the Holy Rude, head to the small knoll which is known as Ladies' Rock; you are now in the Valley Cemetery!

### Ladies' Rock

The Ladies' Rock (**Site 36**) is sometimes said to be where the ladies of the court watched either the jousting in the Butt

Field to the south-west below the Castle (**Site 42**) or the close quarter combat in what is now the Valley Cemetery (the one to the south full of statues). However, John Harrison argues it's more likely to be an older Catholic shrine, Our Lady's Rock. It is absolutely clear that this was one of two cannon positions for Bonnie Prince Charlie's futile last-ever siege of Stirling Castle in January 1746... you'll never guess what happened! The Castle troops watched the Jacobites assemble their material, and then blew them to hell. In the ensuing conflict, Mar's Wark (**Site 24**) lost its roof! The Jacobites' gunpowder store for the siege was at St Ninians, an ancient centre of Christianity repaired by King James IV around 1500. Unfortunately, in their haste to escape the Jacobites blew up their gunpowder store and with it St Ninians, with only the tower surviving! The Smith Museum (**Site 51**) holds an illustrated fan of the explosion!

Come back down from Ladies' Rock and to your left is a monument under glass.

### Solway Martyrs

The most prominent of the monuments in the cemetery is the one under glass with a white angel. This is dedicated to the Solway Martyrs (**Site 37**) and memorialises a story of two young women being tied to stakes at low tide for refusing to acknowledge the authority of Episcopalian Bishops imposed by Charles II in the 17th century. The story was almost certainly made up to help justify some of the actions of the Covenanters.

With the Solway Martyrs to your right, head down the hill and turn right at the second path. There should be two polished granite slabs in the shape of crosses; the one to the right has a single word in Greek: Christian.

## Christian Maclagan

I'm very proud to be an archaeologist and to be a Fellow of the Society of Antiquaries of Scotland, and so it was inevitable that this book would feature Christian Maclagan (**Site 38**), arguably the first female archaeologist in the world (and if anyone wishes to debate this, please email me!). She is the first person to propose that brochs were houses and amongst the first people in the world to record archaeological excavations in a way we would recognise today. Maclagan was not permitted to be a Fellow of the Society of Antiquaries, as she was not a fellow! Indeed, they would not even accept her first major paper unless she had it transcribed by a man! However, while she was a pioneer, she was also a biblical literalist and spent a lot of time and energy looking for evidence of Noah's flood.

Head back to the main path and carry on down the hill to the main cross roads of the cemetery. Take the next path to the right (the statue to Ebenezer Erskine should be to your left) and head to the long line of graves with the large polished grey granite monument in the middle with lots of names; the majority of people buried here died in the Castle.

## Cree Grave

During World War I, Stirling Castle and several big houses in the town served as hospitals for the wounded and in the centre of this long row is a mass grave for 20 soldiers which includes Private Chakasuam, part of the Canadian Forestry Corps and a member of the Cree Nation (**Site 39**). World War I always seems odd and futile to us now, but I feel it was essential to defeat German aggression (the German Kaiser and his generals celebrated the outbreak of war with champagne) and however we feel about war, I think it is always worth remembering the fallen.

Head back to the main cross roads again, this time head towards the three statues – the one in the centre is John Knox. Turn left at Knox and head towards the Ladies' Rock, turn right at the end and then climb the first wee set of steps and head through the first row of graves. You should be in front of a cross to the Moyes family.

### Titanic Engineer
Stirling boy William Young Moyes was the sixth engineer aboard the Titanic and died aged 24 in the sinking staying at his post to keep the lights on; his body was never recovered (**Site 40**). Interestingly his elder brother Alexander Barclay Moyes is also commemorated here, though he's buried in Europe. He fell during the 1918 *Kaiserschlacht* (Kaiser's Battle) when, during World War 1, the Germans deployed a million men on the western front in a last desperate attempt to defeat the allies before the Americans mobilised.

### Martyr's Monument
At the northern half of the Valley lies Scotland's largest pyramid, also known as Salem Rock, the Martyr's Monument or the Star Pyramid (**Site 41**), and it sits just to the south of the Castle Esplanade. Don't worry, there's no King Tut or his curse to terrorise tourists. Designed by William Barclay in 1863 and paid for by William Drummond, the pyramid is the main feature of Drummond's Pleasure Ground and is dedicated to all those who suffered martyrdom in the cause of civil and religious liberty in Scotland. Drummond's handsome polished granite sarcophagus is just to the west. There used to be two bronze eagles on the globes, but these were stolen in the

1960s or 70s. At the base of the pyramid are four marble bibles with the names of religious tracts (short pithy extracts from the bible). These were based on the business of William's brother, Peter, which between 1848 and 1980 had printed and distributed millions of tracts and other tales of Victorian derring-do and morality! The Drummonds had made their money as seed merchants and many of the plants available in his shops were used in the garden!

The point of gardens like this, which combined a nice walk with a touch of Christianity, was to ensure that the working classes had something edifying to do in their free time other than merely drinking and watching football! Indeed, Peter Drummond – of tract fame – was shocked to find people being ferried across the River Forth to Cambuskenneth to visit the Abbey and public houses on Sundays. Gadzooks, that's my weekend cancelled!

With the pyramid to your right, walk to the end of the cemetery and you can either turn right and head up to the Castle (**Site 42**) or turn left then first right and continue along the Back Walk to the royal midden (**Site 11**).

## The Castle

Stirling Castle (**Site 42**; *NS 79077 93978; 56°07'23"N 3°56'48"W*) is one of the finest Renaissance palaces in Europe and does not really need to feature in this book as so much has been written about it already. However, if you do go, think about just how small it really is compared to other castles you've been to. The majority of the Castle and its outer walls are 17th and 18th century. The medieval core, as developed by successive Stuart Royalty from James IV to James VI, comprises a stately square (the Palace, the Great Hall, the Chapel Royal and the King's Old Buildings), accessed from an elaborate monumental gateway, in which the bulk of the Great Hall is presented as an awe-inspiring spectacle of the Scottish Crown's power and taste. The smelly stuff is hidden or off-site: the laundry is likely to have been beyond the Butt Field (**Site 9**), close to Raploch Fire Station, and one of the stable blocks was of course in King Stables Lane... the King's underpants had left the building!

Now I'd like to let you into some things that tend to get overlooked by most tourists and even some of the guides! The first thing to note is that there were at least three Royal chapels; the one still standing is the first Royal Protestant chapel built in Scotland. The one marked on the ground in front of the upstanding one is where Mary Queen of Scots was crowned. The original and oldest one, which dates to the 12th century, lies between the Palace and the King's Old Buildings. This is the oldest element of the Castle, and all that survives from the Battle of Bannockburn. The day after The Battle of Bannockburn, Robert the Bruce was handed the keys to the Castle and he destroyed it to prevent it being used against

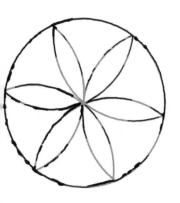

Keep out witches: the King's bedroom's witch mark!

him. It is argued by Peter Yeoman, who supervised the reconstruction of Stirling Castle, that Bruce left the Royal Chapel standing as to destroy it would have been affront to God. Certainly, bodies from the Wars of Independence were recovered from the base of this building.

My final wee secret involves witches, or rather the fear of witches. In the King's bedroom in the palace are two cupboards; the door on the right has a small compass decoration on the other side (i.e. the side that would face a witch attacking the King). This is likely to be an apotropaic mark, designed to ward off witches and malign supernatural forces.

### King James Bible

What is the most popular version of the bestselling book of all time? (Though have you ever tried selling one?!) I am, of course, talking about the King James Bible, which has its roots in Stirling.

The James in question was King James VI, who was Scotland's first Protestant monarch, crowned in our very own Church of the Holy Rude (**Site 26**) in a service by John Knox. James' mum, Mary Queen of Scots, was Catholic and had been deposed in part because of her religion.

James was strictly tutored in Stirling Castle by the elderly and formidable George Buchanan from Killearn (**Site 66**). Indeed, so severe was his schooling that James was terrified by the memory of his former teacher, and notably Buchanan is reputed to have said to King James' obsequious courtiers that while '*you may kiss his arse, I hae skelped it*.' (while you may kiss his bum, I have smacked it!).

The new bible was composed to deal with inaccuracies in older versions and, of course, having a bible that people could read (i.e. not in Latin) was one of the central tenets of the Reformation. James was still King of Scotland when he first proposed the idea, but being King of England gave him the resources to propose this revolutionary new project.

It's hard to describe the overwhelming influence of the King James Bible, but perhaps the most telling compliment comes from arch atheist Richard Dawkins who says that '*a native speaker of English who has never read a word of the King James Bible is verging on the barbarian*'. Why not see if you have a copy lurking on a shelf? Its beauty may surprise you.

### Penny Millar's Slap; King Stables Lane

After you've been to the Castle, if you fancy another adventure, why not walk to the north and take in the view? Stirling Bridge (**Site 48**), the Abbey Craig (**Site 49**) and Dumyat (**Site 78**) are all visible. Just to the left of the white building on the north side of the esplanade is the wonderfully named Penny Millar's Slap (**Site 43**; *NS7916893934; 56°07'22"N3°56'43"W*) (slap is the Scot's word for narrow pass). On the left as you walk down are a series of blocked-up windows and doors. At the bottom you have a choice; you can cross the road and walk round Gowan Hill (the northern half of the Old Royal Park (**Site 12**)) or turn to the right to another narrow lane: King Stables Lane (NS7919993934; 56°07'22"N3°56'41"W).

As you've just come from the Castle, you might note the name of this lane and see, at the bottom of the lane, a series of blocked up arches and doorways: all former entries to the royal stables. The restaurant at the corner of the lane and St Mary's Wynd, The Smithy [20] (home to Stirling's tastiest

---

[20] https://www.facebook.com/thesmithystirling/

Make way for the King's horse: the blocked doors of the royal stables

burgers and best chips in my humble opinion), takes its name from the stable block.

King Stables Lane also marks the original northern boundary of the city which, unlike the southern side, did not really have a substantial wall, just a small one and a steep bank... we really only expected to be attacked from England and not Perthshire or Fife! There was even a gate here (although it was really just a block that was pulled across the road), across St Mary's Wynd, last used in January 1746 against Bonnie Prince Charlie's army – but I don't know if he stopped for a burger!

Now, at the bottom of the lane you are in a wonderful little pocket of preserved medieval Stirling. To the left is the Settle Inn: Stirling's oldest pub, and a very warm welcome. To the right, beyond the Smithy, is John Cowane's House – yes, it's the same John Cowane. The house dates to the 16th century and is a wonderful, magnificent ruin, although at the moment it's not open to the public.

### Irvine Place

On the other side of the road is Irvine Place (**Site 44**; *NS7954193739; 56°07'16"N3°56'21"W*), which also marks the edge of the medieval city, and if you walk down here you will catch glimpses of a massive stone wall to your right, which – while not as big as the wall on the south (**Site 20**) – is still a big wall, albeit serving as a property boundary. Some have argued that the wall may date to the 1650s and Cromwell's invasion.

## Black Friars

If you cross the road at the bottom of Irvine Place, the old city boundary carries on down into Viewfield Street, where it joins with Maxwell Place, which used to be the northern end of Friar's Wynd. There was another gate here, and Friar's Wynd is of course the western boundary of the Dominican Friary known as the Black Friars (**Site 45**; *NS7966093684; 56°07′14″N 3°56′14″W*), because of their black hoods. The Dominicans or Order of Preachers were, and indeed still are, a religious order of the Catholic Church founded in AD 1216 and charged with going out into the community and doing God's work. They arrived in Stirling in AD 1233 at the invitation of Alexander II. The Friary was opposite where the train station is today, and their lands extended down to the Forth. The Friary church was apparently destroyed, or certainly desecrated, in 1560 during the Reformation (the religious revolution from Catholicism to Protestantism) by what must have been the angriest mob in Scottish history who, after destroying churches in Perth, marched the 30 odd miles to Stirling and were still furious enough to desecrate the Blackfriars Church.

The Friary hosted Edward I twice and Murdoch Duke of Albany, who was executed on the Beheading Stone (**Site 14**), was buried here. Excavations by GUARD Archaeology ahead of new flats in 2014 revealed a wealth about the life of the friars and uncovered what may have been a latrine block.[21]

Also, the remains of a likely friar were uncovered. This individual was a young man who died around AD 1271-1320. This means that he could have been in Stirling for the two key battles of the Wars of Independence – Stirling Bridge (**Site 48**) and Bannockburn (**Site 53**) – and could indeed have seen Edward I, Edward II, Wallace and Bruce. At the time of writing, Chris Kane and I – with the help of The Engine Shed and the current Dominicans in Scotland – are planning to re-bury him in the Old Town Cemetery (**Site 28**), and he will be the only known grave of anyone to have potentially wit-nessed the key players of the Wars of Independence.

After Blackfriars you can head north to Stirling Bridge (**Site 48**) or west to Cambuskenneth (**Site 47**), which goes past Stirling's harbour (cross over the bridge to the left of the train station), but just before you get to the harbour is the Engine Shed, a fabby centre all about Scotland's historic build-ings and how we keep them standing (*NS7996993550; 56°07'10"N3°55'56"W*)!

## Harbour

Stirling has always had some form of connection to the sea, although as the size of craft increased they found it harder and harder to get past the rocky outcrops of the Forth, as well as the massive tidal range, and our harbour (**Site 46**; *NS8005993973; 56°07'24"N3°55'51"W*) closed in the 1950s. There are records for trade from the harbour going back to the 12th century and there appears to have been some form of

---

[21] http://archaeologyreportsonline.com/reports/2018/ ARO30.html

wharf at Cambuskenneth Abbey (**Site 47**). As the river is tidal, there are miles and miles of mud, all of which is around a metre deep, and I've been stuck in it myself so please take care if you want to go in the river. In 2018, Stirling Council reinstalled a tidal pontoon at the site of the old harbour (*NS8010593978; 56°07'24"N3°55'49"W*), and this is an amazing place to launch a canoe or kayak. Now, if you fancy being a bit more adventurous there are a set of steps on the eastern side of the Forth at the Old Bridge (**Site 48**), and you can travel downstream from the bridge to the wharf at the old harbour. I've done this several times and, while I've not seen one, I know people who have spotted porpoises here!

## Cambuskenneth Abbey

While Cambuskenneth Abbey (**Site 47**; *NS8087693929; 56°07'23"N3°55'04"W*) is definitely not a secret, it tends to be overlooked as the Castle is so cool. Quite what the name means is unclear: 'cambus' is certainly Gaelic for bend, which makes sense as the site is in a massive meander of the Forth,

Cambuskenneth Abbey from its lost harbour

but Kenneth might be Kenneth MacAlpin who is often identified as the first King of Scotland, or it might simply mean
'muddy'!

The abbey is Augustinian and was founded in the 12th
century AD by our friend David I, as part of his Davidian
Revolution. The Abbey is open and free through the summer,
and is well worth a visit. It was where Robert the Bruce
stored his baggage train for the Battle of Bannockburn (**Site
53**). It features the grave of James III (paid for by his son
James IV, who felt guilty at the role he played in his father's
death at the Battle of Sauchieburn (**Site 54**)). During the mid-
17th century, muskets were fired at a sniper operating out a
window on the western face of the tower, leaving hundreds of
impacts. According to a local tradition (with no other sup-
porting evidence), William Wallace's arm is buried here under
a stone marked W.W. Apparently it had been pulled off the
Barra's Yett (**Site 19**) and patriots place flowers on the spot
every year. On 6th November AD 1314, Robert the Bruce held
his first post-Bannockburn Parliament at the abbey. This con-
firmed that anyone who had not sided with him at Bannockburn was now dispossessed. The children of these people, The
Disinherited, helped the English during the second Wars of
Independence after Robert the Bruce died. The abbey was
dissolved and dismantled after the Reformation in the 16th
century, and some of the stones ended up in Mar's Wark
(**Site 24**).

It was accessed from the east, across the Forth, via a
ford and to the west there was a wharf which was partially
excavated in 2015 (*NS8060593932; 56°07'23"N3°55'20"W*). The
interesting thing about this wharf was that it could not func-

Cambuskenneth Abbey's masonic secret!

tion at today's river levels; the tidal range had to be between 1-2m higher.[22]

Now I will let you in on two genuine secrets. At the base of the tower, in the north-west corner, is a window – and carved into the window frame is a rough sketch of a window. These are probably medieval instructions from a master mason to an apprentice. They were re-discovered after over 700 years by Moira Greig when she recorded all of the different mason marks in the tower. She identified 497 marks from 86 different masons, and not one of them had anything to do with rolling your trouser leg up or the Holy Grail... how disappointing!

The second secret is what's in the upper floors of the bell tower, the best-preserved bit of the abbey. The tower is

[22] http://www.archaeologyreportsonline.com/reports/2017/ARO25.html

normally closed, but I get it opened once a year as part of Scottish Archaeology Month for free! So, if you are in Stirling in September, why not ask me about it? However, just in case you miss it, the tower contains broken ornamental sculpture from the tower (including the worst lion in Scotland), medieval tombstones from the cemetery, and a $9^{th}$ century AD log-boat carved from a single oak tree! The view from the top of the tower is very cool, and indeed the best view of the east of Stirling. At low tide, this view includes the Abbot's Ford to the east.

Now if you are after a biggish walk after the Abbey, head north for the Abbey Craig (**Site 49**) which is very conspicuous... the big tower is a dead giveaway!

## Stirling Bridges

There are actually five Stirling bridges (**Site 48;** *NS7971594573; 56°07'43"N3°56'12"W*) and at least one ford! Everyone knows about the lovely Old Bridge (or Auld Brig, as it's known locally), which is around 500 years old and is

Old Stirling Bridge, around 500 years old and once the biggest bridge in Scotland... from under Stevenson's bridge!

now pedestrianised and which, when it was built, was the biggest bridge in Scotland and the main way north for centuries – used by Mary Queen of Scots and Burns amongst many, many others! As you stand on the bridge with your back to the Castle, the bridge used by William Wallace in AD 1297 was to your left, and at low tide in the summer you can see the gravel bank which surrounds one of the piers. To your right is the Stevenson Bridge, built by Robert Stevenson (the grandfather of author Robert Louis Stevenson of *Treasure Island* fame!), and under this is the likely location of the ford which predates all of the bridges. Beyond that are two railway bridges, built by rival train companies into Stirling who had built two separate and competing lines!

If you look over your left shoulder you will see Mote Hill (**Site 14**) and the Beheading Stone, the medieval execution block of Stirling. One of the most famous people to ap-

The arch that Blakeney destroyed!

parently be executed there was Murdoch, Duke of Albany, who was both the Regent of Scotland during James I's time and his uncle. Murdoch had paid for the repair or construction of either this bridge or its immediate predecessor. He also plotted unsuccessfully against the young James, who had him and lots of family executed for treason – perhaps using the Beheading Stone, meaning it's possible that his last view before he died was the bridge he had helped build... or so the legend goes!

Now, you've heard about General Blakeney partially dismantling the Old Bridge to trap Bonnie Prince Charlie, and the Battle of Stirling Bridge with William Wallace is dealt with elsewhere (**Site 52**). What you may not know is that, where the Bayne's Bakery behind you is, was the location of St Marrokis' Chapel. Professor Richard Oram observes that across Scotland, this saint is associated with the boundaries of burghs and the plague. Records show that during a series of early 17th century plagues where hundreds if not thousands died, the sick and dying were brought to the other side of the bridge and left in wooden huts. While extremely brutal, this was the only way to control infection.

On a lighter note, on the Castle side of the bridge are a series of steps down to the river which is a good way to access the river with a canoe or if you want to go swimming. Now, please note the tidal range here is absolutely huge, between 2-3m, so don't get caught out. There is a particularly nice, deep pool on the eastern side of the bridge, and my daughters and I have been known to jump from the bridge pier. (But please check out the depths and tides, etc., before you go in!)

Choices, choices, choices... from here you can head to Cambuskenneth Abbey (**Site 47**) or back to the Castle (**Site 42**) or to Abbey Craig (**Site 49**).

## The Abbey Craig

At 67m, the National Wallace Monument (**Site 49**; NS8091595640; 56°08′19″N3°55′05″W) is the biggest monument to an individual in Britain, and one of the biggest in the world – and so is absolutely not a secret! I've helped make two TV programmes about the hill and the monument: an episode of *Antiques Road Trip* and one for the Discovery Channel on Stirling, King Arthur and vitrified forts (don't ask!). I've also undertaken a number of excavations across it.

The Abbey Craig (the hill of Cambuskenneth Abbey) has a series of absolutely fabulous views to the west and east. The monument is absolutely brilliant and may have the most impressive view in Scotland from its top... watch out, it gets very windy!

The Wallace Monument and Ben Ledi

Round the back of the monument is another vitrified hillfort (the arcing bank) which was first recorded by Christian Maclagan (**Site 38**), who also left money for the construction of the monument. The Victorians thought that this fort was Wallace's camp ahead of the Battle of Stirling Bridge (**Site 48**). However, the fort is far older and was built to control the Forth crossing; I've dug on it a few times over the years. It was destroyed by fire twice: once between the 5th and 7th centuries AD, possibly by the invading Angles, and again around 900 AD, possibly by the Vikings.

If you've been into the monument you will have seen the famous Wallace Sword which, including the hilt, is 1.63m long. Now, there are a few interesting things about this. First of all, you will have read that Wallace had been betrayed by Sir John Menteith, who received the Earldom of Lennox from Edward I for his services, although John eventually changed sides and backed Robert the Bruce. As a lasting legacy for this betrayal, Menteith had Scotland's only natural lake named after him, the Lake of Menteith (**Site 63**). Really, that's it? One of Scotland's greatest heroes is betrayed and we change a loch to a lake?

So why is the Lake of Menteith a lake? New research by Nick Aitchison suggests that unfortunately it's nothing to do with Wallace. It's to do with the Scots replacing Gaelic and English replacing Scots. In Scots, 'laich' means low lying, so you can have a laich field (the low field) and if you have a big low lying area it can be The Laich, as in The Laich o' Moray. So the Lake of Menteith is actually the Laich o' Menteith or the low lying area of Menteith, which would've referred to more than the lake and probably extended much further across the carse, but because we moved rapidly to English, people thought it was 'lake'. As to why it was linked to Wallace's betrayal, well, that's easy: we needed something to tell tourists!

Anyway, to return to the sword, it's a big sword for a big hero and legend tells us Wallace was a near superhuman figure, so of course he had a big sword. Hmm... there may be some circular logic there. Analysis of the sword reveals it's a composite of at least three swords. So, might the sword be a fake – something to show off to tourists? Well, no, perhaps not. This is the sword that James IV was told was Wallace's, as stored in the Royal Armoury. James IV was after a powerful symbol of the Scottish nation at yet another time of tension with England. I think that when the King asked for Wallace's sword, it either could not be found or it looked a bit rubbish, so they took what was left, gave it a new handle, extended the blade and *voilà*, a heroic symbol, from one of Scotland's greatest heroes, fit for a King!

On your way back down the hill, if you walk to the south-east of the monument, past the vitrified rampart and down the road that the mini-bus drives up (though please watch out for it), you will find immediately to your right one of the quarries used to construct the monument – and if you pay very close attention to the fringes of the quarry you'll spot the last blocks to be quarried, which were never dressed or used in the monument.

At the bottom of the mini-bus road, there is another path to your left (the visitor centre is immediately to your right (*NS8081195729; 56°08′22″N 3°55′11″W*)). This will take you back into Stirling, down over 100 quite steep steps through an ancient woodland... definitely my favourite way to go! There's a good playpark at the bottom, but best of all is Corrieri's [23] – a fabby and very friendly Italian restaurant. I recommend the milkshake, but whatever you do, don't ask for a deep fried pizza (my go-to comfort food... well, I am Scottish!). When I did, I was nearly chased out!

At this point you can head back into Stirling to Stirling Bridge (**Site 48**) if you head south to the Castle, with Abbey Craig behind you, or if you've not been to Cambuskenneth Abbey (**Site 47**) head east with the Abbey Craig to your left!

---

[23] http://www.corrieris.co.uk/

But... slow down. Before you do that, have a look across the roundabout; on the opposite side to Corrieri's is a monument to Scotland's first powered flight.

## The Barnwell Brothers

Scotland's first powered flight!

Frank and Harold Barnwell established an engineering busi-business in Causewayhead in 1907 and built their first plane in 1908. On 8<sup>th</sup> July 1909, they tested a biplane near this spot and it reached 13 feet and flew for eighty yards... Scotland's first flight (**Site 50**; *NS8053295662; 56°08'19"N 3°55' 27"W*). Both brothers carried on flying, but unfortunately both died in test-flights. Bits of some of their planes are kept in the Smith Museum and Art Gallery.

## The Smith Museum and Art Gallery

The Smith (**Site 51**; *NS7908393501; 56°07'08"N 3°56'47"W*) is a wonderful place, full of lovely volunteers, dedicated profes-sionals and a great wee café (the wonderfully fresh scones are my favourite)! I have a close working relationship with the staff so I am in quite a lot. The museum is choc-a-block full of treasures. It features the origins of tartan, the world's oldest football, Mesolithic whale bones from Stirling's lost sea, the world's oldest curling stone, a fan showing the Jacobites blow-ing up St Ninians kirk (**Site 16**), bits of the Barnwell Broth-

THE ANCIENT KEY OF STIRLING

delivered by the Provost and Magistrates to Bonnie Prince Charlie when his Highland Army entered Stirling at 2 p.m. on Monday, 6th January 1746.

Bought at the Bannockburn Sale on 5th October 1960. Lot 107.

Returned to the Provost and Magistrates of Stirling by Captain Charles A Hepburn of Hillhead at 11.30 a.m. on Tuesday, 24th January, 1961.

Bonnie Prince Charlie's key to the Barra's Yett

ers' (**Site 50**) planes, the axe from the last beheading in Britain (**Site 22**) and a key held by Bonnie Prince Charlie (**Sites 19** and **36**). And of course it's an art gallery, so it has an amazing collection and, as of March 2019, a brand new and updated display space!

The founder of the museum had an incredible life and was the inspiration for his friend Robert Louis Stevenson's famous novel *Kidnapped.* Thomas Stuart Smith, born in 1815, was the illegitimate nephew of Alexander Smith who owned Glassingall House near Dunblane. Thomas was sent to France to be schooled and his father paid the fees. However, when his father died in 1831, the fees stopped and Thomas had to teach at the school to complete his education. He returned to Scotland to discover who he was and, while he never met his uncle, his uncle sent him money from time to time. After the death of his uncle in 1849, Thomas spent nine years in the courts fighting for his inheritance. During his time in

Mesolithic whale bones washed up on a long lost shore

Stirling, he founded this wonderful museum and art gallery. Smith's most important paintings feature people of African descent as people rather than servants, which was rare at the time; *Pipe of Freedom*, which is on display, was painted to celebrate the abolition of slavery in America in 1865.

### Whale Bones
At the start of this book, I told you that 10,000 years ago the whole of the Forth Valley was under water and that this coastline was favoured by Mesolithic hunters as there is always something to eat in the sea, including the odd whale. The Smith holds both some of the bones from these whales and the tools used by our ancestors to carve up the carcases!

### Football
The Smith's most famous treasure is the world's oldest football, which dates to the 1540s and was accidentally kicked into the roof of the Queen's Chamber in Stirling Palace and sealed by repairs, where it stayed until 1981 where it was uncovered and then donated to the Smith! Incidentally, this act of generosity still annoys the pants off my colleagues in Stirling Castle, but it's OK as they made themselves a replica. (To quote Nelson from *The Simpsons*: ha ha!)

The world's oldest football!

## Tartan

The most obvious symbol of Scotland, known across the world, is tartan. But did you know its modern origins lie in Stirling? After the last Jacobite Rising by Bonnie Prince Charlie in 1745, the 1746 Dress Act banned the wearing of tartan north of the Highland Line and you could be fined or sent to jail for wearing it! Now of course, Stirling has always been south of the Highlands, so tartan could be made legally here and one William Wilson of Bannockburn was able to make and sell tartan to Scotland south and east of the Highland Line and to the nascent colonies of the British Empire. It was William and family that first started to coordinate tartans and commercially produce them. The Smith holds some of the early patterns and sample books as well as the date stone from the world's first purpose built tartan mill!

## The Last Axe to Behead Someone in Britain

We have already heard of Baird and Hardie and the last beheading in Britain (**Site 22**). Well, the Smith holds the axe, which the curator Michael McGinnes argues was made specifically for the execution and in a bit of a rush, and is thus out of balance. He also says that the cloak used by Mr Young for the execution – which is also in the Smith – features a gash caused by the axe... can you spot it? My

The axe used to behead Baird and Hardie, and Mr Young's cloak

The destruction of St Ninians

friend David Smith (no relation to the Smith of the museum) often gets local children to see if they can spot any bloodstains!

### Fan and Key
The last siege of Stirling Castle was conducted by Bonnie Prince Charlie in January 1746. Though he was given the key to the city gate at Barra's Yett (**Site 19**), it didn't go well and the Jacobites blew up their own gunpowder store at St Ninians (**Site 16**) in their hasty escape! If you look closely you can see 5 people literally blown up into the air above the kirk.

### Plane
Stirling is home to both Scotland's first attempt at flight (**Site 11**) and its first successful powered flight (**Site 50**) by the Barnwell Brothers, and the Smith hosts both one of their propellers and one of their wing frames!

## The World's Oldest Curling Stone

These days curling tends to be undertaken indoors in Scotland as it's the only way to guarantee consistent ice. However, in the past it had to be outside, and the thing about curling outdoors in Scotland is that sometimes the ice is too thin and just when you've made the final, terrific, match-winning throw... the stone vanishes in a soft spot in the ice and no amount of swearing is going to resolve the issue! This is exactly what happened sometime around 1511 when what is now the world's oldest curling stone was lost in Milton Bog! It was found just outside Stirling in the early 19th century when the bog was being cleared.

# The Battles for Stirling

## Stirling's Battles
As you have heard by now, lots of people fought lots of times over millennia to control Stirling: we only know of a fraction of what actually happened, but there were at least eight sieges of Stirling Castle; three vitrified forts and three major battles. Regarding the battles, I won't go into too much detail (though there is a lot!) as you can get that elsewhere and most easily from Historic Environment Scotland's jammed-to-bursting website.[24]

## The Scottish Wars of Independence
You've all seen *Braveheart* and many will have seen *The Outlaw King*. Both are great fun and, while not accurate, do reflect the medieval view of history, i.e. propaganda! The winner really does have the final say and *Braveheart* is no worse than Barbour's *Brus*, written 70 years after the events. Barbour's epic poem doesn't mention Wallace, and it portrays Robert the Bruce's deliberate killing of the Red Comyn – under a flag of truce on holy ground – as an accident rather than

---

[24] https://www.historicenvironment.scot/advice-and-support/listing-scheduling-and-designations/battlefields/

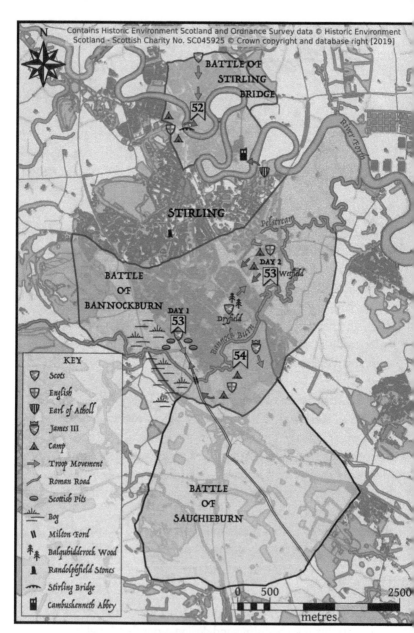

Contains Historic Environment Scotland and Ordnance Survey data © Historic Environment Scotland - Scottish Charity No. SC045925 © Crown copyright and database right [2019]

N

BATTLE OF
STIRLING
BRIDGE

**52**

River Forth

STIRLING

Pelstream

DAY 2
**53** Wayfield

BATTLE
OF
BANNOCKBURN

DAY 1
**53**

Dryfield

Bannock Burn

**54**

KEY

🛡 Scots
🛡 English
🛡 Earl of Atholl
🛡 James III
▲ Camp
➡ Troop Movement
⟋ Roman Road
◓ Scottish Pits
⌇ Bog
‖ Milton Ford
🌲 Balquhidderock Wood
🔺 Randolphfield Stones
〜 Stirling Bridge
🏰 Cambuskenneth Abbey

BATTLE
OF
SAUCHIEBURN

0      500                    2500

metres

Stirling's key battles

a calculated, deliberate and violent act for which he was ex-communicated. Now while you all understand what excom-munication means at an intellectual level, none of you are me-dieval Catholics! To explain, you all know that the sun will rise tomorrow; you don't need to think about it, it will hap-pen, you just know. With excommunication, unless it's lifted you know with a similar certainty that you're going to hell. This also impacts anyone who follows you, and it's no longer a sin to kill them in battle. It's also worth noting Wallace was not a follower of Bruce; he supported John Baliol, the rightful King whom Edward I had stripped of his regalia after the bat-tle of Dunbar in AD 1296, and likely viewed Bruce as only interested in pursuing his own ends – which to be frank is true, it's just that his ambitions eventually aligned with Scot-land's freedom. Now as you have gathered I believe that Bruce was a very, very violent man that at many points was craven and driven by self-interest. However, I also think he was a military genius and Scotland's greatest King.

So, here are the bare bones of the Wars of Independ-ence and please note the 's'; Scotland was at war with Eng-land, other Scots, the Welsh and the Irish between AD 1296 and AD 1328: 32 bloody years. A whole generation was born knowing nothing but conflict. When Scotland's King Alexan-der III died without an heir (remember I said primogeniture was a bad idea?), the Scottish nobility could not decide who had the most legitimate claim and asked their good friend Edward I of England to decide. He demanded to be feudal superior of Scotland for the process and then appointed what many would argue was the weakest candidate: John Baliol (who was backed by the Comyns). Edward then demanded that Scotland support his wars in France. We refused, and signed a treaty with France (the Auld Alliance). Edward invaded and, at the Battle of Dunbar AD 1296, Scotland was defeated. Edward forced John to abdicate (an illegal act) and for all practical and legal purposes Scotland becomes a region of England.

It is at this point difficult to find anything good to say about our then-ruling aristocracy: they have either decided that one King was as good as another and that they might as well swear allegiance to Edward I as long as they kept their lands (and Robert the Bruce is on board with this!). Alternatively, they will have noted that Edward I was old and would die soon and that his son, Edward II, was really not that good. So why not simply wait until Edward I dies and then attack? Which is more or less what Robert the Bruce did!

## The Battle of Stirling Bridge, 11<sup>th</sup> September AD 1297

The first series of rebellions against English rule are generally to do with taxation without representation (sound familiar?). Like any sensible colonial power, you tax the locals to pay for their conquest and for some reason the Scots were unhappy about this. There are a series of small-scale incidents across Scotland, but Wallace leads in the south and Andrew de Moray leads in the north '*and when they got together it was moider!*' (many apologies to anyone who does not remember *Hart to Hart*, but it has been my lifelong ambition to somehow work that into a publication... why not Google it?).

Now, the story of the Battle of Stirling Bridge (**Site 52**; *NS7079004562; 56°07'43"N3°56'08"W*) is better told elsewhere (the Wallace Monument (**Site 49**)), but to keep it short... we won! But have you ever wondered why Wallace won at Stirling Bridge? The story is very familiar; the English camped overnight on the castle side, the Commander John de Warrene slept in, troops advanced and then were recalled, finally they began to cross the narrow bridge and were surrounded on three sides by the Forth, when half the army was over we blocked both the bridge and the narrow point of the meander, trapping the English. The English command was split and poor; they had apparently expected us to wait for them to assemble before fighting, it just wasn't cricket! Really?

The English army controlled the Castle and was amongst the most efficient in Europe. It had just beaten the official Scottish army at Dunbar in AD 1296 and would beat us in again in AD 1298 at Falkirk. This was an unofficial rebellion. We had few, if any, trained knights, our key position was the schiltron – a load of guys with big spears – and all the English had to do was hold on, recross the bridge and go back to the Castle, and yet we overwhelmed them.

Stirling Bridge is important in Scottish terms because it proved we could win, and in European terms it's the first time an army of professional knights was beaten by foot soldiers. So why did we win? The English certainly couldn't explain it.

Our excavations at Cambuskenneth's medieval harbour (**Site 47**) reveal that the Forth's contemporary tidal range was up to 2m higher than it was today, making it twice as wide, and remember all that mud! I think we won because the English panicked. They watched the tide rise and were trapped, the people at the back were pushing forwards, while those at the front were retreating. If an army loses order, it's finished. People fell into the mud and were drowned and crushed. Armour in metre-deep mud is useless! So English panic cost them the battle; they didn't know how high the Forth would rise and order broke down, resulting in the loss of 5000 souls in the cold, clammy mud of the Forth; the greatest ally Wallace ever had!

If you've crossed the bridge from the Castle side, don't make the mistake of thinking the battle was just between the bridge and the railway; the best place to understand the meander is from the rugby pitch on the other side of the railway, which cuts the battlefield in the middle.

As a final aside, and an indication of the absolute brutality of medieval warfare, are the actions of one Sir Marmaduke de Thweng, 1ˢᵗ Baron de Thweng (and that name is not made up!), who was the English keeper of Stirling Castle. He ended up on the wrong side of the bridge and, seeing how the battle was going, rode back across it – ploughing through his own men who either jumped off the bridge or were cut down... what a great leader!

## The Battles of Bannockburn, 23ᵗʰ and 24ᵗʰ June AD 1314

There are two battles of Bannockburn (**Site 53**), Day One and Day Two. Day One is brilliantly told and explored by the National Trust for Scotland's Bannockburn Centre (*NS7953290643; 56°05′36″N3°56′16″W*), and I don't intend to say very much about it. Day Two is a different matter, and is without doubt the most important and astonishing battle in Scottish history.

Here is a summary of the immediate lead-up to the battle: Stirling Castle was besieged and Edward II was challenged to relieve it. Bruce picked Stirling as it's the furthest north of the remaining Scottish castles in English hands and would stretch English resources the most. Ahead of the battle, Robert the Bruce picked a spot where, if he dug a series of pits, he could control the greater numbers of the English army and prevent them from flanking him. However, he only faced a small proportion of the English. The majority spent the day resting, including Edward II who stayed in his tent. There are three key events on Day One: the main conflict is somewhere around the National Trust Bannockburn Centre, there is then a second clash between Thomas Randolph, Earl of Moray and Sir Robert Clifford. Finally, there is a midnight raid by the Earl of Atholl, a renegade Scot with a personal grudge against the Bruce, on his baggage train at Cambuskenneth Abbey (**Site 47**). In effect, Day One could be described as setting a trap for a bully, taking them by surprise and giving them a bloody nose before running away!

As an aside, what has been called The Borestone (destroyed by people chipping away mementoes) is more likely to have been a 16th or 17th century rough out for a millstone. One of the main reasons why everyone got excited about this stone is because Robert Burns, who visited Stirling in 1787, was so moved by our military past at 'The Borestone' that he composed what was arguably his most famous poem – and if you've not read it, it's really good blood and guts stuff!

> *Scots, wha hae wi' Wallace bled,*
> *Scots, wham Bruce has aften led;*
> *Welcome to your gory bed,*
> *Or to victory!*

On a side note, my friend Paraig McNeil, the Gaelic Bard, who knows hundreds if not thousands of poems by heart, always used to say '*welcome to your glory bed*', which he had learned at school. We think the school toned the poem down a bit! As part of the Stirling Heritage App, Paraig and I recorded a guided walk across the whole of the two days of the battlefield combining history, myth and poetry!

However, the really interesting stanza is the last one (which no one ever remembers) which says:

*Lay the proud usurpers low!*
*Tyrants fall in every foe!*
*Liberty's in every blow!—*
*Let us do or die!*

Now, this just seems to be about good, general principles of freedom. However, a closer reading by Professor Robert Crawford of St Andrews University indicates that the poem calls the then-Royal Family the Hanoverians usurpers, and links their overthrow to both the French (Liberty) and the American Revolutions (tyrants). Very dangerous sentiments... remember, in 1820 Baird and Hardie (**Site 22**) were sentenced to being hung, drawn and quartered for treason!

Before talking about Day Two, I want to briefly return to the clash between Randolph and Clifford. Local legend has it that this took place at a pair of standing stones in a house called Randolphfield, which is next to a house called Cliffordpark (*NS7946892476; 56°06′35″N 3°56′23″W*). Tradition has it that these were erected to commemorate the battle.

Now, I was sceptical about this as Scotland is full of legends and everyone likes to connect things – it always makes for a better story! So I thought it was more likely that these were either modern stones put up in someone's garden for a good story, or perhaps they were prehistoric and that the tale was later pinned to the stones. According to my colleague Douglas Scott, the stones themselves are on a lunar alignment, so this supported a prehistoric origin. So I thought, why not do a small dig to see if we could get dating evidence? My colleague Fiona Watson (the archaeologist, not the historian) and I did just that in 2014. This excavation revealed no modern material in the foundation cut of the stone, ruling out a modern origin, but recovered charcoal dating to AD 1283-1396, i.e. contemporary with the Battle of Bannockburn. This means that the stones are not prehistoric and could in fact be a memorial to the clash, and therefore the oldest Scottish War Memorial!

I said above that Day Two is far more important than Day One, and there can be no question about that. But why is that and where was it? The English army outnumbered the Scottish army, they were better equipped, and most of them had not fought the day before. The main Scottish formation to this point, a static schiltron, is only effective against cavalry; it's absolutely useless against archers. If the English army could get mobile they would outflank the Scots and decimate them as they did at Falkirk in AD 1298 to poor old Wallace. Day One was characterised by careful planning and preparation over months by the Bruce. By contrast, the tactics for Day Two had to be decided overnight. The great historian of the Bruce, Professor Geoffrey Barrow, openly criticised him over the decision to fight Day Two at all. If Bruce fell, the Scottish cause was lost, it was all ended and there was no Wallace to start things up again. However, remember that Bruce was not the rightful King; that was still John Baliol. Also, as we have heard, Bruce had been excommunicated for the killing of the Red Comyn – and although this had been lifted, there was still a question over his leadership. If he failed, with what was his biggest ever army, his leadership might be challenged. So he had to fight, he had to gamble all and of course he won, and that is why he is Scotland's greatest King and an absolute military genius. So what did he do? It's very simple: he turned static schiltrons into dynamic ones, so that the men with spears moved in sync with each other. Now this is far, far harder than it sounds, and will have taken months to learn. Dr Fiona Watson (the historian not the archaeologist), has argued that as the numbers of people wishing to join the army continued to grow, those that had not been trained were excluded from the fighting and were left in camp at Coxet Hill (**Site 15**), as without training they would hamper the army's movements. These people were known as the Sma' Folk and, according to tradition, they played a very significant role in the events of Day Two.

So having established revolutionary Scottish tactics, the next thing the Bruce had to do was pick the ground. The English had camped overnight on low lying ground between the Pelstream and the Bannockburn (*NS814019 1747; 56°06'13"N 3°54'30"W*), and the Scots approached through the Balquhidderock Wood which is on a raised ridge (*NS808649 1123; 56°05'53"N 3°55'00"W*) to the south-west of the English camp. This has led to two different theories: the Dryfield and the Wetfield. The Dryfield theory suggests that the Scots let the English climb the slope at Balquhidderock and then engaged them, while the Wetfield theory argues that the Scots marched down the slope and engaged the English. Now, the presence of battlefield objects in the Wetfield area does not change anything, as following the battle the English army scattered and objects could be dropped anywhere.

In my opinion, the key factor is the English army's numerical superiority. If they got to the Dryfield, they would surely have flanked the Scots, whereas if the Scots marched to the English, the geography of the two burns would hinder the English army's movements. In effect, the Scots could push the English cork back into its bottle. This would create a classic panicky crowd where people would be crushed and the English become their own worst enemy.

Accepting that the battle took place on the Wetfield, it would have become very clear to the English that they were losing, but this was no big deal at this point. If they could undertake an ordered retreat to the west, they could shelter in the Castle, which they control, and more importantly the siege would be lifted. It was at this point that the Sma' Folk played their part. Remember: these people wanted to fight, but were likely barred as they had not been trained. Tradition says that, seeing how the battle was going, they wanted to get stuck in. Now of course, all of this could simply be a poetical conceit to illustrate how all sections of society were involved in the defeat of Edward II, but it certainly makes sense. The Sma' Folk approached from Coxet Hill (**Site 15**) in the north-west, and to the already-wobbly English they look like a fresh army, blocking their escape route to the Castle... oh 〚*expletive deleted*〛! At this point, order breaks down and the defeat becomes a rout. It is this that transforms the nature of the Scottish victory.

The Scots focused their attention on the nobility and either capturing them alive or seizing their corpses. The English King narrowly escaped, after being turned away at the Castle and charging round the predecessor garden at the King's Knot (**Site 8**). The reason for the Scottish focus on the nobility is that every knight or earl or duke was both the head of a large estate and the primary agent of government and the military. So if they were captured, their estate was deprived of leadership. If the individual was then ransomed, the estate would bankrupt itself trying to pay – this argument also applies to corpses. The money raised from these actions supported the army and Bruce then used it to launch raid after raid after raid on northern England, each time demanding protection money. Bruce's plan created chaos and impoverished the north of England, ensuring there was little or no appetite to go back into Scotland. But it took 14 years of this raiding before the peace treaty was formally signed in AD 1328 at the

Treaty of Edinburgh. Bruce died the year after, and England started the second Wars of Independence!

Immediately after the victory, Stirling Castle (**Site 42**) was surrendered to Bruce and he destroyed it to ensure it could no longer be used against him, leaving only the chapel standing so as not to insult God, who had obviously forgiven him and condemned the English!

One final note about our angry, aggressive friend Sir Marmaduke de Thweng, 1$^{st}$ Baron de Thweng, one of the 'heroes' of the Battle of Stirling Bridge. He was also at Bannockburn and personally surrendered to Robert the Bruce, who let him go as he was in a generous mood!

On another final note (hey... there's a lot to get through!), Edward II was so confident that he would win that he brought a poet, Robert Baston, with him to compile an epic account of his glorious defeat of the rebellious Scots! Instead, he was captured by the Bruce, who made him write an account of the true battle and then just let him go. This poem, an eye-witness account of the battle, is fabby, and a modern translation of it was made by Scotland's First National Makar (poet) Edwin Muir for the reopening of the Scottish Parliament. Intriguingly, the poem is not triumphalist, but it is gory! Its strongest theme is the futility of conflict and is well worth a read!

### Battle of Sauchieburn, 11$^{th}$ June AD 1488

We don't really know very much about this battle (**Site 54**; *NS8083190154; 56°05'21"N3°55'01"W*) as it was effectively a royal coup. James III was violently deposed by an army led by his son, the future James IV. The official account of the battle simply states: on this day the late King fell on the field of Stirling. The King is dead, long live the King!

However, there are still a few things to say about it. Coal Hill, the likely location of James III's muster point (which is my favourite view of Stirling), demonstrates James III's incompetence. He was carrying Robert the Bruce's sword and just thought if he echoed Bruce's tactics at Bannockburn he would win. Except of course, that Bruce's initial position was to the west of the Bannockburn, forcing the English to cross it, while James crossed the Bannockburn to engage his enemy and gave up any geographical advantage... d'uh!

The best view of Stirling!

The next thing to note is that many people have heard the later tale that James III fled the fighting to the ford at Milton, where his horse was startled by a woman gathering water and James was thrown. He then staggered to a nearby mill and was welcomed into the house, where the locals summoned a priest – who promptly killed the King! Now, all of this is nonsense and it was made up to demonstrate three things: James III was a coward; James IV had nothing to do with it; and anyway, it was all the fault of those nasty Catholics and isn't the Reformation a really good idea?

Of course, at this point James IV was Catholic, as was Scotland, and he was genuinely horrified that he had played a role in his father's death and so was driven to a series of acts of penance. He wore an iron belt around his waist to mortify his flesh, he reendowed Cambuskenneth Abbey (**Site 47**) as a suitable mausoleum for his father, he helped rebuild the Church of Holy Rude (**Site 26**) after a fire, he invited the Grey Friars to Stirling (the High School (**Site 21**) was built over the Friary), and he spent money on St Ninians (**Site 16**). In addition to this he also transformed the Castle (**Site 42**) and the Royal Park (**Site 12**), built Europe's biggest ship (the *Great Michael*), conducted magnificent jousting competitions in the Butt Field (**Site 9**), paid for research into flight (**Site 11**) and was all-in-all Scotland's greatest peace time King. But he threw it all away – including his life – in 1513 at the Battle of Flodden, losing a battle he should have won, as he had more troops and better equipment! Flodden was an attempt to open a second front against England while Henry VIII was invading France. James' body was never recovered and his tomb at Cambuskenneth Abbey – where he had planned to rest with his father, reconciled in the afterlife – was dismantled and used by someone else. This was an enormous blow to Scotland and is lamented in the song the *Flowers of the Forest*, whose lyrics by Jean Elliot simply state that: *'The pride o' oor land lie cauld in the clay'.*

# Beyond Stirling

## EAST

### Plean Country Park

Plean Country Park (**Site 55**; *NS8275486826; 56°03'36"N 3°53'04"W*) is well worth a visit, but the main reason for recommending it is that it has some upstanding World War I practice trenches in it (*NS8258186656; 56°03'30"N 3°53'14"W*). Park in the car park, and head south along the eastern fringe of the park. Immediately after crossing the burn there are a series of lumps and bumps and hollows... these are the trenches! There's also a nice bun shop in Plean called Alex Graham's.

### Torwood Broch

Torwood or the Tappoch (**Site 56**; *NS8333884980; 56°02'36"N 3°52'27"W*) is the biggest and best preserved broch around Stirling (although it's just in Falkirk). There is a signposted walk to the site, which is built within an older hillfort. It has the area's oldest staircase and the clear remains of a stone ledge that supported an upper floor. The Roman road that runs to Ardoch (**Site 83**) in the north and Rome in the south is just to the south of the site. I dug here in 2014 and we identified another bank to the hillfort and recovered Neolithic material from a much older settlement built here before the

The 2000 year old staircase at Torwood broch

broch and hillfort. When you walk in, imagine a low ceiling and a dark interior. The staircase is to your left. Now as you walk up the stairs you will have passed what may be an Iron Age shrine. Turn around, squat down and look for the reused face-down cup-marked stone; use your hands to feel for it if you can't squat. The broch is 2000 years old and the reused stone may be 4000 years old. Now, there is a lot of evidence for Scottish Iron Age rituals taking place in dark, cramped conditions, with the sensory deprivation creating an almost hallucinogenic effect. The staircase where you find the hidden cup-marking is the darkest and smallest space in the broch. I imagine that we are looking at a secret, to be revealed to members of the community as they come of age, something that would bind the generations together – and if you find it, perhaps, in some way, you too are connected with them!

The ancient cup and ring marked stone at Torwood, perhaps reused to create a shrine?

## Cowie Stones

You might not believe it but Cowie (**Site 57**; *NS85522881.83; 56°04'22"N 3°50'26"W*) is an ancient place and sits on raised land just above the ancient, now lost, inland sea. Excavations in the 1990s revealed Stirling's oldest house, and to the east of the village at Castleton Farm are a huge cluster of cup and ring marked stones, each one prettier than the last and all 3-4000 years old! Access is tricky, so park at the eastern end of Ochilview in Cowie (*NS84362888.97; 56°0444"N 3°51'34"W*) and take the tarmacked path to the north. (Don't try to take the track to the east which, while marked on the maps, is no longer usable... my friend Therese and I went that way first and got soaked!) It's a 15-20 minute walk in. There are several plaques, but the best two are at Foxhead Farm and Castleton Wood. To get to the first one, walk up east towards Foxhead Farmstead, and access the gate at the sharp left turn

(*NS8575488585; 56°04'35"N3°50'13"W*); then turn right via the next gate and the approach the scrubby area to your left from the north and in the middle you will find five carved circles (*NS85878840; 56°04'29"N3°50'06"W*). To get to Castleton Wood, retrace your steps to the crossroad and then head south to the wood at the top of the slope. Climb the fence on the left (*NS 85436 88298; 56°04'25"N3°50'31"W*) and in the middle of the scrubby woodland (*NS8551988162; 56°04'21"N3°50'26"W*) you will find six carved circles.

Stirling's most beautiful cup and ring stones (Foxhead and Castleton)

### The Pineapple

What is the biggest piece of fruit in Scotland? There was a time when pineapples were amongst Scotland's most exotic foods (they still are in my house!), and if you could grow them (in elaborate hot-houses) you were seriously wealthy. In 1761 the Earl of Dunmore built a series of greenhouses with a building in the shape of a pineapple as the central feature (**Site 58**; *NS8889188542; 56°04'36"N3°47'12"W*), and each time I visit it takes my breath away... and it's free! (Though it's just outside Stirlingshire, in Falkirk!)

### Keir Hill of Gargunnock

Just to the immediate west of Gargunnock Kirk (a lovely wee church well worth a visit) is Keir Hill of Gargunnock (**Site 59**; *NS7066094329; 56°07′27″N 4°04′56″W*), an odd wee knoll, which my friend Therese McCormick and I excavated in 2016. Believe it or not, this is the site of a native defended fort that was here when Gargunnock was part of the Roman Empire. There is nothing to see, but you can stand where Roman Legionaries stood and traded with the locals!

### Leckie broch

There's no parking near Leckie broch (**Site 60**; *NS6926693998; 56°07′15″N 4°06′16″W*), so you have to park in Gargunnock and walk in. It's a very nice walk, albeit a bit

My youngest daughter Heather, on Leckie broch wall above the elaborate stone carvings!

muddy! I've mentioned Leckie before, as a broch that was probably destroyed by the Roman Army. It sits on a tiny rocky outcrop, and the burn that created the knoll has lots of fast flowing gullies and pools and is well worth the walk in its own right.

The eastern side of the rocky outcrop is covered with cup-marked stones and carvings and is the biggest plaque of such carvings in the whole of Stirling.

After Gargunnock but before the track to the Hole of Sneith (**Site 60**), if you fancy a break... the Woodhouse [25] is a wonderful and quite stylish restaurant and a great farm shop!

### Hole of Sneith

I always struggle to describe the Hole of Sneith (**Site 61**; *NS6551793082; 56°06'41"N4°09'51"W*). It is a waterfall on the Boquhan Burn, within a cavern on a geological fault. If you approach it from the west, the burn simply vanishes into the earth. But if you come from the east, after a serious scramble you are presented with a fantastic natural cathedral of a space, with 10-15m high cliffs and a 10m high waterfall. The roar of the waterfall echoes round the cavern and there is a seductively calm pool at the base, in which I've had a discreet, private – if bracing – dook!

This was also one of the locations where a local Church of Scotland minister hid while being hunted by the authorities. Though why was a minster on the run? Had he fiddled the books? What exactly was going on? The late 17th century in Scotland is known as the Killing Times. Church of Scotland Ministers were arrested and executed, others led armed rebellions against the state who had passed laws against specific

---

[25] https://www.thewoodhousekippen.co.uk/

The gorgeous Hole of Sneith

types of Christian worship and assembly, which were then broken up by armed troops.

This incredible situation happened between 1661 and 1689, when around 100 executions for treason are recorded. The first of these was James Guthrie, Minister at the Church of The Holy Rude, who is commemorated in the Old Town Cemetery and whose head lay on a pike in Edinburgh for 27 years! The Smith Museum (**Site 51**) holds some of his personal possessions.

Following the Restoration of Charles II in 1660, the Westminster Government began to exert increasing control over the way Christianity was practised in Scotland, in direct breach of the National Covenant signed between the Church of Scotland and Charles II, which secured the freedom of the Scottish church in exchange for military support for him. The supporters of the Covenant are known as the Covenanters and their acts of worship, which were banned by law, were known as conventicles. Every year in commemoration of these acts of resistance, an open air sermon is held at Kirk o' Muir (**Site 73**) in the Carron Valley.

It was the Minister in Kippen, James Ure, who hid at the Hole of Sneith after he led 200 armed volunteers from Stirling to the Battle of Bothwell Brig in 1679. Following their defeat, Ure went on the run and a reward of £100 was offered for his capture! His wife and children were held for questioning, as was his mother who eventually died in Glasgow Tolbooth. Ure was subsequently pardoned and is buried in Kippen.

This persecution finally ended when James II was replaced by his daughter, Mary, and her husband William of Orange in the Glorious Revolution of 1689... James II's grandson was, of course, Bonnie Prince Charlie, but that's another story!

## The Carse and The Moss Lairds

Earlier we heard of the inland sea around Stirling and how it gradually became a bog. Well, the peat in this bog was up to 18 feet deep and while there was always some small scale agriculture in it, generally it was perceived as a vast, useless bit of land. Most people have heard of the Clearances, where brutal landowners forced tenants from their ancestral land and sent them packing abroad, most often to Canada. While we might dispute precisely what happened, it was the last phase of something called the Improvement Period, where traditional farming methods were overturned and production increased over 300% in 100 years. In Stirling, the biggest transformation was the draining of the Carse (**Site 62**; *NS6481797890; 56°09′16″N 4°10′41″W*), which after the Ice Age was an inland

Flanders Moss, courtesy of Mr Stuart Innes

sea. Traditionally, this is started by Lord Kaimes of Blair Drummond in 1787 who constructed a massive water wheel to drain the bog. However, much of the clearance work was undertaken by people derogatorily called Moss Lairds. However, as Moss Lairds are recorded on maps by the mid-18th century, it is likely that the process was already underway. The peat was so deep that the Moss Lairds carved houses out of it. Such was the scale of the peat clearances, which went on until the 1860s, that it was claimed to have poisoned the valuable salmon fisheries in the Forth in what may be one of the world's first large scale pollution disasters, and a Royal Commission was launched.

Flanders Moss, the biggest surviving element of the Carse, is now a nature reserve and features a lovely boardwalk to explore right into the heart of the bog.

### Inchmahome Priory

Inchmahome Priory (**Site 63**; *NN583420I017; 56°10′50″N 4°17′01″W*) sits in the middle of the Lake of Menteith, the lake named after the villain who betrayed Wallace

Inchmahome Priory from the air, courtesy of Mr Kenneth Halley

(**Site 49**). The priory is well worth a visit, but the most exciting bit for me is the ferry out to the island, which is run by the ever-pleasant staff from Historic Environment Scotland!

### The Spout of Ballochcleam and Carleatheran

While we have the right to roam, we can't just leave our cars anywhere, so before this next site here is a little note about parking... park to the west of Bailie Gow's Bridge and walk up towards Easter Glinns farm, and then follow the track up the valley.

Another word for waterfall is spout, and the wonderfully-named Spout of Ballochcleam (**Site 64**; *NS6524292219; 56°06'13"N 4°10'06"W*) represents the start of the Boquhan Burn, which goes on to carve the Hole of Sneith (**Site 61**). It's a small, perfectly-formed waterfall. But the real reason to come here is the view to the north. The path gradually climbs and, with every step, you gain more and more of a view. At the top, you have a series of fantastic choices. You can continue to head south along the wind turbine tracks (one of the lovely things about them!) to the Carron Valley and John De Graham's Castle (**Site 74**), or you can turn east and head towards Carleatheran (*NS6878891849; 56°06'05"N4°06'40"W*).

Carleatheran is a prehistoric burial cairn – just like the one that held Torbrex Tam (**Site 3**) – situated at the highest point on the northern fringe. I'm not sure about its name. The first element might either be *caer* or *carr*; both are Gaelic and the first means fort and the second rock. Now, Gaelic really stopped being used around here at least 700 years ago, and we don't know what was in our ancestor's minds when they saw this cairn. Perhaps they thought it was an old fort or just a big rock. Why not go and make up your own mind?

If you are really keen, head south-east after the cairn and join up to the shooting tracks (there's a gap of about 2km), and then you can either walk to Cambusbarron past a series of reservoirs or down the slope to Gargunnock and Keir Hill (**Site 59**) – if you have a bike, the latter is definitely a total rush!

## The Clachan Oak

If you've driven to or from Balfron, you will have passed what at first glance appears to be a scabby oak tree, held together by iron bands (**Site 65**; *NS5473489251; 56°04'26"N4°20'07"W*). The next time you go that way, stop and have a look at what might be Stirlingshire's oldest tree. The tree looks a bit sad as it's beginning to stag (which is when the upper crown begins to die and the tree retreats into itself, to create a lower crown), but it is very much alive!

'Clachan' is the medieval term for hamlet or village and Balfron Clachan is the oldest part of Balfron, which is also why the church is there. The tree is probably 4-500 years old, so was here when our James VI became James I of England. It was there when Cromwell's troops captured Stirling Castle, and when Bonnie Price Charlie's troops failed to! It was seen by one of our greatest architects, Balfron's very own Alexander 'Greek' Thompson (all the benches in Balfron echo his designs), and thousands and thousands of other people over its long life!

The iron bands, however, are grimmer. They're not designed to hold the tree together and, in fact, have probably damaged it; they are part of a set of jougs and were once commonplace across Scotland. They were designed to secure local miscreants to the tree via a metal collar, so that they could be subject to public ridicule. The practice ended in the late 18th century, apparently after a woman was left too long in them, tripped, and was strangled to death!

Also make sure you stop at the lovely The Bakers and More [26] on the main street, which has the best Danishes in Stirlingshire!

### Killearn

Killearn (**Site 66**; *NS5227385975; 56°02'38"N4°22'23"W*) is a lovely wee place, with a fantastic café (The Three Sisters [27]). It is also the birthplace of George Buchanan, tutor of both

---

[26] https://www.tripadvisor.co.uk/Restaurant_Review-g1489508-d3467752-Reviews-The_Bakers_More-Balfron_Scotland.html

[27] https://www.threesistersbake.co.uk/killearn/

Mary Queen of Scots and James VI, who also taught in France and Portugal. He was the intellectual force behind the deposition of Mary Queen of Scots, and is Scotland's best medieval Latin poet. He is commemorated with a very impressive 103 foot tall obelisk built in 1788 – it's right next to the church in the centre of the village... you can't miss it! Now, medieval Latin poetry is not something that you can easily dip into, but Buchanan's is well worth it. Fortunately for us, the lovely Robert Crawford has translated many of them, and they are great fun. My favourite extract describes his bitter fury at Beleago, a colleague in Portugal who denounced him to the Catholic Inquisition for suspected heresy. Buchanan was arrested, imprisoned and interrogated and very, very scared. This extract makes his feelings clear, and is addressed to his former colleague:

'*Server-up of venison sludged from pig's ball,*
*Thrice winner of the Nobeleago Prize,*
*For out-Cretaning Cretans with his Course in Creative Lies,*
*Cretinous silly-git syllogist, philosobutcher, Zeno of Lard,*
*Exhibitionist, inquisitionist, circumcisionist,*
*Throatslitter, nestshitter, brainsquitter, inkspitter, G and*
*Inquisitor's Portuguese Libyajewish Supergrass who grassed*
*Me up, got me arrested, tested, tortured, chucked*
*In prison, that Magog of goats and groats,*
*That Papal brown-noser, that Sniffer-out-of-Heretic-in-his-own-Sandals'*

While you're in Killearn, make sure you visit Killearn Glen, accessed from Beech Drive (stop at Heron House Nursery (*NS5230885555; 56°02'24"N4°22'20"W*)) and the delightful Ladies's Lynn (*NS5217285331; 56°02'17"N4°22'28"W*), which is the only surviving feature of the 18$^{th}$ century designed landscape surrounding the 17$^{th}$ century Place of Killearn (that's what big houses in Scotland were called!). It's a manmade waterfall, set in a wee yew tree grove. This is the sort of place where the gentry might recite poetry and drink tea (which was very expensive at the time)! One final note: immediately after the Jacobite '45 rising, the garden was redesigned in the shape of the Union Jack... absolutely no way of mistaking the owner's politics!

### Finnich Glen

Finnich Glen (**Site 67**; *NS4960884900; 56°02'00"N4°24'55"W*), the key feature of which is the Devil's Pulpit, is an absolutely fabulous deep, twisty, turny gorge that has been made famous by *Outlander* (Liar's Spring) and gets up to 30,000 visitors a year. Unfortunately, at the time of writing there is no infrastructure or parking, which has resulted in at least one death from people parking badly. The only steps down to the glen are on the south side, but are in a very poor state of affairs and should not be attempted by anyone who is not fit, confident and wearing good boots with ankle supports. I would not recommend parking anywhere near the site; rather, start in Killearn (**Site 66**) and take the time to walk down, following the burn and be prepared to get wet. (I took my shoes off and rolled up my trousers the last time I went!)

When you head north-west I recommend a quick stop at the Blair Drummond Smiddy [28] (toilets, great café and a tasty butcher with a wonderful selection of pies and other treats!).

### Doune Castle

Doune Castle (**Site 68**) has become a bit of a tourist trap these days; lots of cars and lots of *Outlander* fans, and absolutely no sign of Jamie! However, I would still recommend visiting, but I am going to suggest a nicer walk in – and Doune itself is a wee gem. Park just to the north of the nearly 500 year old Spittal Bridge (*NN72175012284; 56°11′13″N 4°03′40″W*) and then cross the road to the bridge side. Walk up the hill

The nearly 500 year old Spittal Bridge

---

[28] https://www.blairdrummondsmiddy.co.uk/

where the entrance to the path is just on the right, heading east along the footpath to the River Teith and then along the footpath at the bottom of the valley. Make sure you look back at that wonderful bridge!

However, before you start walking, look up the slope to the conifer woodland. Believe it or not, you are looking at the boundary of James VI's royal hunting forest, built at the end of the 16th century. This is also the start of a lovely meandering walk to Old Kilmadock (**Site 69**) to the west. A wee extra for Doune, General Sir Ian Hamilton – who organised the disastrous WWI amphibious assault at Gallipoli – is also buried close by in Deanston's Kilmadock cemetery (*NN7167100701; 56°10´54˝N4°04´08˝W*); a village which of course has produced some wonderful whisky.[29] And if you're a fan of military history, you won't want to miss the memorial to Sir David Stirling (*NN7555700322; 56°10´45˝N4°00´23˝W*), who founded the SAS (Special Air Service). Finally, you may notice all the signs to Doune feature a pair of crossed pistols; this is because in the 17th and 18th centuries Doune was home to a series of famous gunsmiths, and it's often said that the first shot fired in the American War of Independence was one of theirs! All this and more is explained in the wonderful Kilmadock Heritage Centre (Doune's museum).[30]

### Old Kilmadock

Old Kilmadock (**Site 69**; *NN7065402484; 56°11´50˝N4°05´11˝W*) is one of the birthplaces of Christianity in Scotland, and amongst the most beautiful locations for a

---

[29] http://www.deanstonmalt.com/

[30] https://doune.co/

cemetery in Scotland. It's a lovely walk from either the Moray Estate Offices (*NN7068603056; 56°12'09"N 4°05'10"W*) or Spittal Bridge (*NN7217501284; 56°11'13"N 4°03'40"W*), and the cemetery and path are maintained by the wonderful ROOKS (Rescuers of Old Kilmadock)... big shout-out for Ro, Peter and the gang! In 2018, my friend Sue Mackay recovered a piece of skull which had eroded from the boundary of the cemetery, which showed evidence for a sword wound... arggg! Now, one of the things a local council archaeologist is responsible for is reporting when human bone turns up (which happens more than you might expect!). Well, I phoned the police to say don't worry, it's old and not a murder victim. Anyway, an hour later two burly and very suspicious policeman rang my doorbell to ask me about the human remains I had 'found', and I could see the suspicion in their eyes. *Okay*, I said, *no problem – they're upstairs on the dining table*. They looked

Old Kilmadock, one of the cradles of Scottish Christianity

at each other and I swear I was literally seconds away from being pinned to the ground while they got the cadaver dogs into the house! However, all was revealed and they stayed for a wee chat... phew!

## Callander

Callander (**Site 70**) is the gateway to the Highlands and well worth a visit: it's full of quirky wee shops and great places to eat! But if you twist my arm and are after a recommendation for a uniquely Scottish treat, I'd suggest a deep fried pizza from Bruno's on Main Street – make sure you get it with lots of salt and lots of sauce!

It has two lovely hillforts (*NN6494207873;56° 14′ 39″ N4°10′52″W and NN6014707585;56°14′25″N4°15′29″W*), a Roman fort (*NN6130207858;56°14′35″N4°14′23″W*), and Scotland's largest long cairn, measuring an incredible 322m long and 15m wide: Auchenlaich (*NN6495707338; 56°14′22″N4°10′50″W*). The cairn sits in a caravan park, so I'd suggest parking in Callander and walking along the cycle way.

## Loch Lubnuig and St Bride's

As well as being very pretty, Loch Lubnuig (**Site 71**; *NN5857310613; 56°16′01″N4°17′07″W*) is also incredibly accessible. It has a car park and it's literally a minute or two to the loch, which is another of our favourite places to swim and canoe. Best of all, there is a prehistoric crannog in the middle of the loch (an artificial island which had a timber house on it; Google 'Loch Tay crannog'). Watch out, though; after a few steps the shallow margins give way to a much deeper and colder middle. Remember: stay calm, get your breath, float on your back, work out where you are, and swim for the closest shore!

To the south of the loch, on the left as you come from Callander, is the ancient chapel and cemetery of St Brides (*NN5850709819; 56°15'35"N4°17'09"W*), which contains some Early Christian stones and is the ancestral burial ground of the McKinleys, ancestors of the 25th President of the USA.

After Loch Lubnaig, you're less than two hours from Oban, which is the sea food capital of Scotland, as well as some of the most amazing beaches in Scotland. As my wife says, west is best!


## SOUTH

### North Third and Swallowhaugh

Two of my favourite hikes (and please note, they both have rough ground and some steep slopes!) are around the North Third Reservoir (**Site 72**), which was built in 1911 to supply water to Grangemouth. It's a wonderful walk. Start at the southern end (you can park here (*NS7581887901; 56°04'04"N3°59'47"W*)) and follow the path as it winds through an ancient beech woodland, and slowly but surely climbs the hill; the view to the west to the source of the Bannockburn is fantastic. There is a small prehistoric hillfort on the path at the northern end of the hill (*NS7628 8933; 56°04'51"N3°59'22"W*), and a very steep climb down the northern end through Windy Yett Glen. This northern end is the most interesting, as it features the wonderful infrastructure of the dam in all its Art Deco splendour! The walk along the western shore of the reservoir is nice and easy, and the water is full of wild fowl!

If you are still after an adventure, head west along the Bannockburn into a once-booming industrial landscape associated with lime production. As you move along the burn, you will see a series of limestone layers which the burn has exposed and which was targeted for quarrying from the Medieval Period onwards. Further up the burn you will see lots of circular mounds; these are clamp kilns, used to turn limestone into quicklime for either fertiliser or for use as clay mortar on buildings. All of the smaller clamp kilns were abandoned in the late 18th century for ever-larger lime kilns, the biggest of which, the Murrayshall lime kiln (*NS77049 93053; 56°06′52″N 3°58′44″W*), was built around 1850 – it even had its own tram line. As you head further up the burn, keep your eyes peeled for fossils from the lost 300 million year old shallow sea that once lay on the equator.

## Kirk o' Muir

One of my favourite drives and – if I'm brave and it's warm, cycles – is from Stirling up and down into the Carron Valley. You could be anywhere in rural Scotland, though the narrow road reminds me of the Hebrides. Certainly you need to take time, show courtesy and not be distracted by the amazing landscape. If you're travelling west from Carronbridge to Fintry, the first thing you pass is a small stone-built enclosure.

This is the medieval cemetery of Kirk o' Muir (**Site 73;** *NS7007084008; 56°01′53″N 4°05′12″W*), which dates to the 14th century and was abandoned in the 17th century, when the area was used for illegal conventicles (Christian worship of a type the authorities did not like, and actively repressed with soldiers!). Every year local churches hold a conventicle to commemorate the battles for religious freedom. In the 19th century, the cemetery was the site of Scotland's smallest school (the foundations are still there), which was described in an official report as a hovel!

But what really interests me is the early 19th century iron cage, the mort safe. This is not an anti-zombie device (before you ask): it was designed to stop the bodies being dug up. By this point you've already heard about grave robbing undertaken for medical experimentation (**Site 34**)! It's a bit tricky to park at, but there is a windfarm bellmouth just to the west.

Guaranteed to stop all grave robbing: the mort-safe at Kirk o' Muir

## John de Graham's Castle

After Kirk o'Muir (**Site 73**) but before the Loup o' Fintry is Sir John de Graham's Castle (**Site 74**; *NS6813785848; 56°02'50"N 4°07'07"W*), which dates to the 13th century. It may be associated with Sir John de Graham, who fought with Wallace at Stirling Bridge (**Site 52**) and who is buried in Falkirk (*NS8874479997; 56°00'00"N 3°47'08"W*). The castle sits on the shores of the Carron Reservoir, and the easiest way to it is from the wee unnamed road just to the west. The castle is no longer upstanding, but was a variant of a motte and bailey. The motte part is dug into a glacial mound and appears to still have upstanding footings for timber buildings and, if this is the case, it may be the best preserved timber castle in Scotland! If you want to see a reconstruction of a medieval village,

I would try Duncarron village just on the other side of the reservoir.[31]

## Loup o' Fintry

In Scotland 'loup', pronounced 'lowp', means to leap or jump and it's normally associated with a gorge and some kind of superhuman event. Some of these legends appear to have pre-Christian origins, though they are also associated with Wallace or the Jacobites – people achieving massive leaps to escape the English! Just to the west of John de Graham's Castle (**Site 74**) is the Loup o' Fintry (**Site 75**; *NS6604786376; 56°03'05"N 4°09'08"W*), which is a 94 foot high waterfall. There is not much parking and the rough track is not for anyone who can't handle uneven ground, but it's well worth it, especially the view to the west.

The Loup o' Fintry, courtesy of Mr Stuart Innes

---

[31] http://www.duncarron.com/dun/

## Logie Old Kirk

Logie Old Kirk (**Site** 76; *NS8152996975; 56°09'03"N3°54'31"W)* has been mentioned a few times. It's a wonderful 17th century ruined kirk with a heap of amazing and intricately-carved stones (park next to the new church (*NS8178296620; 56°08'51"N3°54'16"W)* and walk up the hill). The graveyard is maintained by the Friends of Logie Old Graveyard Group (of which I'm the chair), but all the hard work was done by Joe and Eleanor Young and kudos to them!

I've already mentioned the Viking hogbacks which are meant to be houses for the dead. One was smashed up by a local workman but has been partially reassembled, and if you crouch down by the complete one you can still see the carved shingles. But I never explained what the name meant: Logie is Gaelic for hollow, but in the context of an early church, Professor Thomas Clancy from Glasgow University has argued

Vikings were here: the Logie hogbacks

that it's a corruption of 'locus', Latin for 'place', which in turn is short for Holy Place. Professor Clancy goes further and argues that this logie reflects the Pictish takeover of Stirling in the $7^{th}$ and $8^{th}$ centuries AD, and was an attempt to impose their version of Christianity on the locals.

Logie is dedicated to St Serf, who was active in the $7^{th}$ or $8^{th}$ centuries AD. One of St Serf's miracles from around Logie concerns a stolen sheep (still a big deal in Stirling!). The suspected thief had denied all knowledge and was then asked to swear on the saint's staff and, as he did, the sheep bleated from his stomach. Now, whether or not this really was a miracle or just very bad indigestion I will leave you to ponder!

The prominent rocky hill to the east is known as Carlins Crag (witch's hill), and some people claim this is where suspected witches were thrown off to see if they could fly (in which case they were a witch). Surprisingly, there are no recorded cases of witches being detected here. Others suggest that this was where the witches met the Devil for an overnight party (sounds a bit like teenagers to me!). However, at this spot in the late $18^{th}$ century an elder from Logie Kirk claimed to have shot the Devil with a silver coin (I thought that was werewolves?). When he and the minster went to the spot, all they found was someone's pet goat!

To my mind the most beautiful monument in the cemetery is that of Margaret Clason, the wife of James Bryce, who died on the $14^{th}$ March 1716; her gravestone took almost a year to make! James Bryce was a wealthy merchant, who had three wives and 15 children. Many of the current descendants of Margaret and James now live in Holland! James lived in the nearby village of Pathfoot, which is now gone except for his house, Blawloan (*NS8047096993; 56°09'02"N 3°55'32"W*), which is the oldest in Bridge of Allan. The house still has his marriage lintel on it (*17 JB JK 31* (from a subsequent wife)), which was considered rather ostentatious by his neighbours!

## Craigarnhall

We have heard about Septimius Severus and his invasion of the early AD 300s. All Roman invasions used marching camps; temporary camps where they stayed overnight. While camps across the entire Roman Empire were all constructed on the same basis, the Severan campaign ones were different. All of them had an annex where the Imperial Family was likely to have stayed. At the site of the Craigarnhall (**Site 77**) camp, it's possible to follow in Severus' footsteps to this day (the centre of the annex is at *NS7595798245; 56°09'38"N3°59'56"W*), although the area has now been ploughed flat. The other reason that these camps were different is that, at this point in the Roman Empire, the functioning capital of the Empire was where the Emperor was and not

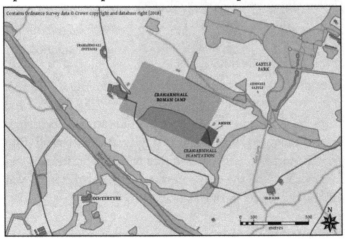

The capital of the Roman Empire (for a day or two):
Craigarnhall marching camp

Rome. So, for a couple of days around 300 AD Stirling was the capital of the Roman Empire.

### Dumyat

Stirling is full of brilliant views, but Dumyat (**Site 78**; *NS8326697366; 56°09'17"N3°52'51"W*) is the absolute best. It also happens to be an Iron Age vitrified fort, although the fort is just to the south-west on the hill called Castle Law.

The Fort of the Maeatae, the view to Dumyat

The easiest way there is to come from the west; there's a car park (*NS8129297998; 56°09'35"N3°54'46"W*) and an excellent surfaced path for most of the way. Dumyat is *Dun Maeatae*, which is Gaelic for *The Fort of the Maeatae* – the tribe mentioned by the Romans as living here around AD 200, and the ones who Emperor Septimius Severus conquered when he was staying at Craigarnhall (**Site 77**). The fort has been vitrified (see Mote Hill (**Site 14**)) and if you walk round the main rampart, (the band of stones), you will see lots of cool vitrified stone.

### Dunblane

If you come to Stirling, you have to go to Dunblane (**Site 79**; *NN7813601440; 56°11'24"N3°57'55"W*). Not only does it have

Sir Andy Murray's Golden Postbox, an amazing Cathedral (with incredible medieval carvings in it), Scotland's oldest purpose-built library (The Leighton Library, 1684) and a great wee museum, but it also has two wonderful butchers opposite each other (though which has the tastiest pies? You'll have to try them both!). So, a few wee secrets about Dunblane. First of all, it used to be called Nrurim, and its name was changed to Dol Blaan (the plain of Blain) after Viking raids on the Isle of Bute forced monks to relocate St Blane's relicts from the monastery to here! King Aed, the son of Kenneth MacAlpin, was assassinated here in AD 878. The western doorway of the Cathedral is covered with musket ball impacts from an unrecorded siege. Finally, the Cathedral claims to have two $8^{th}$ to $10^{th}$ century AD Pictish symbol stones from the early monastery associated with St Blane... they don't; the stones have no Pictish symbols on them. They are contemporary to the Picts but are, however, far rarer – they are carvings made by Britons, who were first invaded by Angles and then by Picts and who in protest burnt their own houses in around AD 850.

## Paradise Pools

Paradise Pools, or The Devil's Bucket (**Site 80**; *NN81886o1048; 56°11′14″N3°54′17″W*), is a favourite of my daughters. We go there two or three times every summer. It's an absolutely incredible, deep gorge in the Wharry Burn in the middle of the Sheriffmuir Battlefield. Every year, we watch the sand martins in the river bank as red kites and buzzards circle overhead, every now and again a heron passes, and if you go in late September there's heaps of hazelnuts. Lying still, you can watch trout fry in the peaty brown stream. There's no pollution, and I always drink straight from the burn. But my favourite thing is the swimming. Now, you must explore and carefully check this for yourself, and don't dive here. If you get it right, there is a natural water slide for 10 metres, which ends in a plunge in an 8-10 feet deep pool, but you have to land just right or you will break an ankle! I tend to park near the MacRae Monument (*NN8151701948; 56°11'43"N3°54'40"W*) and walk along the Beauly Denny track.

## The Gathering Stone

To the north of Dunblane is the Sheriffmuir Battlefield. The battle was a key element of the 1715 Jacobite Rising, and a miserable affair which ended in a draw – effectively a Jacobite loss, as they never managed to seize control of Stirling. Eye-

A terrified soldier's lost spoon!

witness accounts from the time describe redcoats fleeing from the highlanders, running down toward the Wharry Burn (and of course Paradise Pools (**Site 80**)). You can certainly imagine their terror as they flee for their lives, dropping their bags and weapons as the howls of the Jacobites grew closer. In 2018 a head of forestry, my friend John Gooder, organised a metal detection exercise of the area over which the redcoats ran, and one of the objects uncovered was a broken spoon with King William's symbol (WR (William Rex) and the crown) marked on it (yes, that King Billy!). And guess who found it...? Jimmy Bain!

The Jacobites were led by one of the Earls of Mar (**Site 24**) and funded by silver from the Ochils. To the north is the Atlantic Wall (**Site 82**) and then slightly beyond that again is Ardoch Roman fort (**Site 83**), the best-preserved timber fort in the world!

Anyway, one of the key features of the battlefield is the Gathering Stone (**Site 81**; *NN8109002184; 56°11'51"N3°55'05"W*) which, according to legend, is where the clans gathered before the battle, though no-one really believes that. The stone is far older and of prehistoric origin. It was knocked down by troublemakers working on the railway, hoping to upset the locals, and the landowner subsequently covered it with an iron grille to protect it. But why was the stone so important? Well according to local tradition it was also known as the carlin or beltane stone. Carlin is Scots for witch and Beltane, or Bealtaine, is one of two traditional early Celtic divisions of the year, the other being Samhain. Summer ran from May Day to Hallowe'en and winter from Hallowe'en to May Day. Bealtaine is associated with May Day, and Samhain with Hallowe'en.

Research by Kay Muhr demonstrates that across Scotland and Ireland, Bealtaine was associated with bonfires, rituals associated with cattle and milk, and meetings of chiefs. Many have associated the rituals with worship of the God Béil, but it might also simply be connected with 'good fire'. On balance, the fire element seems to be key, and gradually through the 17th and 18th centuries the practices became more and more circumscribed, and the tradition simply becomes a chance for cowherds and young people to meet in the hills and have a party – which was still recorded at Callander towards the end of the 18<sup>th</sup> century. In Scotland, the older name for the Gathering Stone is one of the few remaining Bealtaine place names, and certainly a tradition of assembly is implied in its modern name. Might the Gathering Stone be an ancient place of fire worship?

## The Atlantic Wall replica

If you like Nazi Megastructures (and be honest, who doesn't?), then you'll know Professor Tony Pollard of Glasgow University. I have shamelessly stolen one of his better lines for this next site. (He doesn't mind, as he's a good egg!) The end of the Nazis started here... this top-secret research and training ground was used in the preparation for D-Day, one of the most important events in world history and the largest ever invasion!

Following the Nazis' occupation of Europe, Hitler ordered the construction of a massive series of defenses along Europe's coastline, often using slave labour. A key element of these was the infamous Atlantic Wall designed to repel tanks. They were constructed from reinforced concrete, at which the Germans excelled.

In order to determine how to breach these walls, in 1943 the British formed the Anti-Concrete Committee. The plans for the Atlantic Wall were smuggled out of occupied Europe in a biscuit tin. The British then constructed a series of replicas across Britain to test methods of breaching them, and the biggest and best preserved of these is at Sheriffmuir, Stirling. Sheriffmuir was chosen both for its relative isolation and its proximity to the major transport hub at Stirling.

The complex of reconstructions reflects both German offensive and defensive positions, and recreates the ground conditions and distances from the landing craft in the sea all

All three of the Cook girls at the Atlantic Wall!

the way to the wall. The Atlantic Wall at Sheriffmuir (**Site 82**; *NN8377803657; 56°12′41″N 3°52′31″W*) is a massive block of reinforced concrete 86m long, about 3m in height and up to 3m thick. As it was used for target practice, it's covered with hundreds of missile impacts. If you close your eyes you can almost hear the explosions, feel the shocks and smell the gunpowder!

My favourite element is the Tobruk Shelter, which is to the immediate east of the wall and is based on the German tactic of burying tanks in sand, leaving only their main gun barrel exposed. The shelter develops this idea into two fixed gun positions and an underground shelter.

There was a long history of military training at Sheriffmuir. Originally named 'The Sheriff Muir', it was used for medieval weaponshaws. In World War 1 the ground was laced with practice trenches, which were constructed by the

52nd (Lowland) Division who trained on the range before going to Gallipoli in 1915, and the majority of these are still visible. Infamously, many of these troops were killed in the Gretna Train Disaster on the 22nd May which resulted in the deaths of over 200 people and is still, to this day, Britain's worst train crash.

Captain M.A. Philip (Brigade Signals Officer, 185 Bde 3 Div.) was involved in the Wall's construction. He recollected:

> '*We began some Combined Operations exercises, pretty primitive at first, known as 'dryshod-exercises'. A road or some other suitable landmark represented the coastline, and if you were on one side of it you were technically afloat and on the other side on land again. Men and vehicles were fed across the 'coastline' at specified intervals to represent landing craft discharging their contents*'.

If you intend to visit the site, please note that the ground is very uneven so watch your footing! Finally, there is a lot of broken and snapped iron rebar, so be very careful when you explore the remains.

### Ardoch Roman Fort

The best-preserved Roman Fort in the world... wow! (**Site 83;** *NN8391409918; 56°16'03"N 3°52'33"W*) Say it again, say it loud, say it proud! There is parking on the left just after the bridge at the end of Braco, but it is a very busy road so watch out. Roman legionary forts were the same over the world, and were all meant to end up the same way. The fort was built to secure a victory, there was a civilian settlement around it of camp followers (traders and prostitutes!), and in turn fields developed around the fort to feed the troops and it became a population centre. Locals, when there for work or trade, gradually became Romans. The soldiers retired and were given land locally, they married, and their children may have signed up to the army and ended up in a different province, building new forts. The civilian settlement gained legal rights and became a city. Manchester, Lancaster, York, Carlisle... all started the same way, and if the Gask Ridge hadn't been abandoned, Ardoch would have ended up a city.

The site sits above a river valley and is surrounded by nine sets of banks and ditches, each of which would have bristled with spikes. Inside would have a been a mini-city, wooden barracks, hundreds of men, all getting on with their lives but living with the constant threat of attack. When you go, have a look for Agricola's parrot. No, it's not a Monty Py-

The view to Agricola's parrot at Ardoch and the wilds beyond the Roman Empire!

thon style corpse in a cage; it's the name given to the curving parrot beak shaped ditch on the north entrance, which is found on most of Agricola's constructions. There is also a very stylish coffee and bun (Braco Coffee) shop in Braco, the wee village next to the fort!

# Further Reading

THERE is a lot written about Scotland and not all of it is any good! If you want to learn more about the Wars of Independence, I would recommend *Under The Hammer: Edward I and Scotland* by Fiona Watson and for Bannockburn in particular, *Bannockburn 1314: A New History* by Chris Brown and *Bannockburn 1314-2014: Battle And Legacy* edited by Michael Penman. An excellent introduction to Scottish early history and archaeology is *Scotland After the Ice Age: Environment, Archaeology and History 8000 BC-AD 1000* edited by Kevin Edwards and my old professor Ian Ralston; after that, anything in the New Edinburgh History of Scotland series. If you are mad keen on early Scottish history and archaeology then I'd suggest anything by the following: Dennis Harding, Ian Armit, James Fraser, Alex Woolf, David Breeze, Sally Foster, Gordon Noble, Richard Oram, Ian Ralston, Kenny Brophy, Alison Sheridan and Fraser Hunter... who are all exceedingly good eggs!

# Closing Thoughts

IN an age of austerity, archaeology and history seem like luxuries. They're not education, the NHS or social work. No one will die without them, and I agree – they are the expensive bells and whistles of a civilised society, which is precisely the point! If you're lucky enough to be employed as an archaeologist or a historian, I think there is a burden on you to demonstrate to society that it's a price worth paying and that Scotland would be a poorer, more mundane place without them. I aim to meet these high standards one day!

I also think that without a true understanding of the past, it risks being misinterpreted and becoming propaganda, spread by unscrupulous politicians and demagogues who would turn us against each other. I am Scottish and a patriot, but as proud of Wallace as I am of Churchill; both fought for freedom against ruthless aggressors. The past is yours and you have an obligation to learn from it, but this also means that you have a right to explore it, to get involved and to contribute. So, what's holding you back?

If you're in Stirling, email me at **cookm@stirling.gov.uk** to come and get stuck in. Outside Stirling, you can join the wonderful people of Archaeology Scotland and outside Scotland, the Council for British Archaeology.

# Acknowledgements

S
O if you bought the book, thanks! If you visited Stirling, I hope you enjoyed it and will come back soon, if you're a local taxpayer, many, many thanks! You pay my wages and I hope you think I'm worth it!

Thanks are also due to the lovely Andrea Cook who edited my dire prose and puts up with me on a daily basis; to Stirling Council Archives and the wonderful Pam McNicol, Stirling Council's Archivist for permission to reproduce both James VI's and Bonnie Price Charlie's letters to Stirling's Provost. Polygon Books gave permission to quote from *Apollos of the North: Selected Poems of George Buchanan and Arthur Johnston* (2006), Robert Crawford's translation of Buchanan's verse.

The Smith Museum and Art Gallery gave permission to reproduce photographs of their objects. The ever-generous Professor David Breeze provided a copy of Ptolemy's map. The very talented Emily McCulloch gave permission for the use of Torbrex Tam image. Mr Kenneth Halley gave me permission to reuse his fabby image of Inchmahome Priory and Mr Stuart Innes gave permission for his very evocative images on The Loup o' Fintry and Flanders Moss.

The original concept for the book was stolen from my friend David Connolly, who is trying to do one for East Lothian, but is far too busy having fun. My friend Ian McNeish introduced me to the fine people of Extremis Publishing, Tom and Julie Christie. Chris Kane and Jim Roche have always been good companions in the pub and wonderful sources of encouragement and detail about Stirling! The patient and diligent Therese McCormick (who is fluent in the obscure language of Murray-ese), also edited the text and produced the maps, all uncredited illustrations and the two main Cowie cup and ring mark stone images. All the other photographs are the copyright of the author, unless otherwise stated and any mistakes are of course tests to see if you've been paying attention.

# Image Credits

The illustrations in this book are sourced from the personal photographic collection of the author, with the exception of the following images which are detailed below:

Images of the world's oldest football (page 114), the St Ninians fan (page 116), the ancient key to the Burgh of Stirling (page 116), the executioner's axe and cloak (page 115) and the whale bones (page 113) are Copyright © The Stirling Smith Art Gallery and Museum, all rights reserved, and are reproduced by kind permission of the copyright holder.

Images of the James VI correspondence (page 67) and Charles Edward Stuart correspondence (page 71) are Copyright © The Archives of Stirling Council, upon whose premises the original documents reside, and are reproduced by kind permission of the copyright holder.

Images of the Stirling sites map (page 7), Stirlingshire sites map (page 9), map of Stirling's key battles (page 120), map of Craigarnhall marching camp (page 157), the Cowie cup and ring mark stone (page 16), the Roman Stone transcription (page 54) and the witch mark transcription (page 97) are Copyright © Therese McCormick, all rights reserved, and are reproduced by kind permission of the copyright holder. The Roman Stone transcription is after RCAHMS Stirlingshire 1963, 399. Edinburgh.

# About the Author

Dr Murray Cook is Stirling Council's Archaeologist and is from Leith originally, though he also lived and went to school in Edinburgh. He lives in Stirling with a long-suffering wife, three teenage girls and two pesky but loveable cats. He has undertaken numerous excavations across the region and published over 40 books and articles. He won a Stirling's Provost Award in 2018 for his work for the Council, where he has helped raise over £300,000 to be spent on community archaeology and research and has even got invited to see the Queen at Holyrood Palace, along with a few hundred others! He has appeared on several TV programmes, and has sometime even been paid! He writes a regular column in the Stirling Observer and runs Stirling Archaeology a Facebook page dedicated to Stirling's fantastic heritage!:

https://www.facebook.com/Stirling-Archaeology-176144165815143/

Murray studied at Edinburgh University worked first for AOC Archaeology, rising from subcontractor to Commercial Director. His PhD, which has a rather long and boring title, was based on 10 years of research in Aberdeenshire on settlement patterns between 2000 BC and AD 1000:
https://www.scottishheritagehub.com/content/case-study-kintore-aberdeenshire-shining-light-black-hole

He is an Honorary Research Fellow at Stirling University, a Fellow of the Society of Antiquaries of Scotland, runs an occasional course at Forth Valley College on Stirling and likes to do it in ditches (archaeology that is!). He also co-runs regular training digs open to all under the name Rampart Scotland:
http://www.rampartscotland.co.uk/

Archaeology is at first glance an off-putting word, easy to say but hard to spell and Murray has been called the Council's Archivist and Architect before. But he believes that archaeology should be open to all, it is our shared past and it belong to everyone, so barriers should be removed. On this basis Murray runs a series of free walks, lectures and digs through the year to allow people to explore their past and its open to everyone... email Murray to join: **cookm@stirling.gov.uk**

Also Available from Extremis Publishing

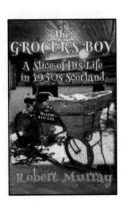

# The Grocer's Boy
## A Slice of His Life
## in 1950s Scotland

### By Robert Murray

The 1950s in Carnoustie: a beautiful seaside town on the Tayside coast, and a place which was to see rapid social and technological advancement during one of the fastest-moving periods of cultural change in recent British history.

In *The Grocer's Boy*, Robert Murray relates his account of an eventful childhood in post-War Scotland, drawing on fond memories of his loving family, his droll and often mischievous group of friends, and the many inspirational people who influenced him and helped to shape his early life.

Join Robert on his adventures in retail as he advances from his humble beginnings as a delivery boy for the famous William Low grocery firm, all the way to becoming the youngest manager in the company's history at just nineteen years of age. Read tales of his hectic, hard-working time as an apprentice grocer — sometimes humorous, occasionally nerve-wracking, but never less than entertaining.

From Robert's early romances and passion for stage performance to his long-running battle of wits with his temperamental delivery bike, *The Grocer's Boy* is a story of charm and nostalgia; the celebration of a happy youth in a distinctive bygone age.

# Exploring the NC500

## Travelling Scotland's Route 66

### By David M. Addison

Travelling anti-clockwise, David M. Addison seeks his kicks on Scotland's equivalent of Route 66. Otherwise known as NC500, the route takes you through five hundred miles of some of Scotland's most spectacular scenery. No wonder it has been voted as one of the world's five most scenic road journeys.

There are many ways of exploring the NC500. You can drive it, cycle it, motorbike it or even walk it, even if you are not one of The Proclaimers! And there are as many activities, places of interest and sights to be seen along the way as there are miles.

This is a personal account of the author's exploration of the NC500 as well as some detours from it, such as to the Black Isle, Strathpeffer and Dingwall. Whatever your reason or reasons for exploring the NC500 may be, you should read this book before you go, or take it with you as a *vade me-cum*. It will enhance your appreciation of the NC500 as you learn about the history behind the turbulent past of the many castles; hear folk tales, myths and legends connected with the area; become acquainted with the ancient peoples who once lived in this timeless landscape, and read about the lives of more recent heroes such as the good Hugh Miller who met a tragic end and villains such as the notorious Duke of Sutherland, who died in his bed (and may not be quite as bad as he is painted). There are a good number of other characters too of whom you may have never heard: some colourful, some eccentric, some *very* eccentric.

You may not necessarily wish to follow in the author's footsteps in all that he did, but if you read this book you will certainly see the landscape through more informed eyes as you do whatever you want to do *en route* NC500.

Sit in your car and enjoy the scenery for its own sake (and remember you get a different perspective from a different direction, so you may want to come back and do it again to get an alternative point of view!), or get out and explore it at closer quarters – the choice is yours, but this book will complement your experience, whatever you decide.

# Travels in Time
## The Story of
## Time Travel Cinema

### By Colin M. Barron

Since the earliest days of cinema, time travel movies have enthralled and amazed audiences across the world. With their tales of changing history and exploring possible futures, time travel cinema has repeatedly challenged critical expectation and proven popular with moviegoers the world over.

In this exciting new study of the genre, Colin M. Barron explores the history of the time travel film from its formative period right up until the present day. Examining the golden age of time travel movies and their glory days in the 1980s through to the most recent features to have emerged in the past decade, he discusses the many elements which have made these films among the most memorable in all of science fiction cinema.

Recounted with sharp wit and a keen eye for detail, *Travels in Time* is the essential guide to the past and present of time travel movies, with more than a few hints of what we can expect from the future of this endlessly fascinating category of film.

# Contested Mindscapes
## Exploring Approaches to Dementia in Modern Popular Culture

**By Thomas A. Christie**

Dementia is a mental health condition which affects an estimated 50 million people worldwide. Yet it has, until recently, been an unfairly neglected subject in popular culture.

*Contested Mindscapes* considers the ways in which the arts have engaged with dementia over the past twenty years, looking at particular examples drawn from the disciplines of film and television, popular music, performance art, and interactive entertainment.

Examining a variety of creative approaches ranging from the thought-provoking to the controversial, *Contested Mindscapes* carefully contemplates the many ways in which the humanities and entertainment industries have engaged with dementia, exploring how the wide-ranging implications of this complex condition have been communicated through a variety of artistic nodes.

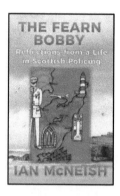

# The Fearn Bobby
### Reflections from a Life in Scottish Policing

### By Ian McNeish

'It's all about the community', the words of Kenneth Ross, Chief Constable of Ross and Sutherland Constabulary, guided Ian McNeish through thirty years of police service. They were true then, back in 1974, and they are true now.

Ian held a police warrant card for three decades, serving communities across Scotland. In that time, his work saw him moving from the northerly constabulary where he policed the rural Hill of Fearn to the social challenges that presented themselves amongst the urban landscape of Central Scotland.

From his formative years in post-War Scotland through to his application to join the police service, Ian has led a rich and varied professional life that ranged from working in iron foundries to building electronic parts for the Kestrel Jump Jet and legendary Concorde aircraft. But once he had joined the police service, he found himself faced with a whole new range of life-changing experiences – some of them surprising, a few even shocking, but all of them memorable.

Leading the reader through his involvement in front line situations, Ian explains the effects of anti-social behaviour and attending criminal court appearances, in addition to dealing with death and the responsibilities of informing those left behind. He considers topics such as ethics, public interest, police and firearms, drug issues, causes of crime, and a lot more besides.

In a career where his duties ranged from policing national strikes to providing comfort and support through personal tragedies, Ian advanced through the ranks and saw first-hand the vital importance of effective management and good teamwork. Whether as the 'Fearn Bobby', policing a remote countryside outpost, as a seconded officer working for the Chief Executive of a Regional Council, or as a Local Unit Commander in Bo'ness, Ian always knew the importance of putting the community first. Comparing to-day's policing techniques with his own professional experiences and examining both the good times and the harrowing pitfalls of the job, his account of life in the force is heartfelt, entertaining, and always completely honest.

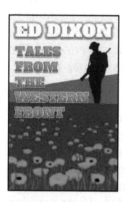

# Tales from the Western Front

## By Ed Dixon

*Tales from the Western Front* is a collection of stories about the people and places encountered by the author during more than three decades of visiting the battlefields, graveyards, towns and villages of France and Belgium.

Characters tragic and comic, famous and humble live within these pages, each connected by the common thread of the Great War. Meet Harry Lauder, the great Scottish entertainer and first international superstar; Tommy Armour, golf champion and war hero; "Hoodoo" Kinross, VC, the Pride of Lougheed; the Winslow Boy; Albert Ball, and Jackie the Soldier Baboon among many others.

Each chapter is a story in itself and fully illustrated with photos past and present.

For details of new and forthcoming books
from Extremis Publishing, including our
podcasts, please visit our official website at:

# www.extremispublishing.com

or follow us on social media at:

www.facebook.com/extremispublishing

www.linkedin.com/company/extremis-publishing-ltd-/

Lightning Source UK Ltd.
Milton Keynes UK
UKHW020617170919
349930UK00007B/23/P

9 780995 589797